For Sedonia Palace

with all good, strong wishes

and love.

Sh

Sheila L. Levicman

Austin, Texas

June 23/06

Jelly Is Where You Find It

Jelly Is Where You Find It

A Biographical Anatomy of a Poem

Donald Weismann

www.ivyhousebooks.com

PUBLISHED BY IVY HOUSE PUBLISHING GROUP
5122 Bur Oak Circle, Raleigh, NC 27612
United States of America
919-782-0281
www.ivyhousebooks.com

ISBN: 1-57197-459-8
Library of Congress Control Number: 2005909047

Printed in the United States of America

To William A. Arrowsmith, Roger W. Shattuck and John R. Silber, who first discovered "Jelly Was the Word" while it was still written in longhand over forty years ago.

In the winter of 1962, I was living in Florence, in a villa on the Via Montughi, one of the roads that runs toward Fiesole. The foundation of the villa was laid down before Michelangelo died. It was a big place with seventeen rooms, furnished as if from the tag ends of a few poor provincial museums. The warmest room in the house was a small one on the second floor, and that winter—at least for six weeks of that winter—I found myself in that room almost continuously. I'd arrived in Florence from Genoa that October and the country and the villa looked beautiful in the still pleasantly warm sun. I'd never been in Florence before and I was overwhelmed by what I saw and by what I knew it meant. For a while, that fall, I walked day and night over Florence. I got to know the banks of the Arno for miles, both ways from the center of town. I looked at what Michelangelo had left and Gianbologna and Botticelli and Brunelleschi. I looked at what Dante had looked at and Ficino and the Medici and I was saddened with thoughts of my weak and uncertain talent, my increasing age, and by the obvious shortness and precariousness of life. So, by January, I had in some way given up and retired to that small warm room on the second floor of the rented villa. There was one large window in that room and it gave to an olive orchard across the way. Beyond that I could see a few two-story buildings that may at one time have been villas with that particular Florentine yellow stain on the sides, the generously overhanging eaves, and the dull-red tiles. Beyond that, and before the hills, lay some factories and behind it all, there were railroad tracks, and I could hear the trains running down those tracks, day and night, blowing that high-pitched whistle. I spent a lot of time at that window. From a distance, I got to know a lot of people. I hung a microphone out the window and recorded conversations, parts of conversations, of people passing in the street below. And listening to those voices now, I hear them holding out against that high-pitched train whistle, way out beyond the red-roofed villas. The six weeks I spent in that room were something altogether like the skein of late hours before bed, when you feel petitioned to do something but cannot discover what that something is.

I remember it was Saturday, the 13th of January 1962, about ten in the evening and well after dinner that I found myself, again, in that second floor room of the villa. It looked very neat. Everything—books, painting materials, writing paper, pencils and pens, the typewriter, typewriter paper and carbons, envelopes, stamps, calendar, clock, tape recorder—everything was in place. Had things been out of order I might have spent the evening just putting them in order. Had I a dog in Florence, I might have started picking ticks off him. I looked out the window, I smoked, I studied my hands, picked my teeth, and started a letter I never finished. And then I remembered a time some sixteen years before when, right after the war and still in uniform while on terminal leave, I'd gone to Mexico, telling myself that I was going to write and illustrate some children's books and maybe make a lot of money. I remembered sitting in a room in Ciudad del Maiz on the road that runs between El Mante and San Luis Potosi, and I remembered very well not being able to get started. I stared at the typewriter, which was not the one I'd brought to Mexico. The one I'd brought had been stolen from my room by my friend, a captain of the highway motorcycle police, one night after we'd been drinking together and he brought me home to the casa de huespedes, saw me to bed and sped off with my brand new Smith-Corona and my navy uniform—shoulder boards, ribbons and all. The typewriter I then had was borrowed from the one other English-speaking person in town, Santiago Cunningham. When he'd learned that I'd lost my typewriter, he dug up his own, which he hadn't used in at least a decade, and offered it to me. He said he'd just cleaned it, and that it ought to work well. I hadn't used the typewriter as yet; I just sat there staring at it. I turned it over and looked at its undersides to find hair and bits of fingernails in a matrix of dust. So for the next two hours I cleaned

Santiago Cunningham's typewriter, and after it was cleaned I rolled a sheet of paper into it. It worked all right.

Now ordinarily when I write, I write in longhand and then I rewrite in longhand and when whatever I've written feels right to me I type it out in the clear. But on that particular night sixteen years before Florence, in the village of Ciudad del Maiz in Mexico, I began on the typewriter. More by whimsy or the spirit of a solo game, I decided that I would start with a simple statement and then type as fast and as long as I could, either about that statement or wherever the language, thinking and the machine would take me. The statement I wrote at the top of the page was this: all things are good in the beginning. I skipped four or five lines below that and started to type. I'd told myself that I wouldn't stop to think, figure out, or make grammatically correct, or to clean up odd connections or anything like that. I aimed to keep typing as long and as fast as I could, continuously. After I'd covered about ten or twelve pages, I quit and read what I'd written.

It's been a long time ago and I really can't remember very much of what was on those pages, but I do remember that there were references to Conestoga wagons, to the Garden of Eden, to Daniel Boone in Kentucky, to the buffalo on the plains, to childhood, to the sources of unpolluted rivers, to love affairs and innocence. I don't know what ever happened to those ten or twelve or fourteen pages but I do remember that the following day, about midway through the day, I was started on a children's book, and that some months later—I think it must have been something like nine months later, after moving from Ciudad del Maiz to Ajijic on Lake Chapala—I'd completed nine children's books—illustrations, title pages and all. Only one of them ever saw the light of day. It was published under the title *Some Folks Went West*, and it came out fourteen years after it was written. The others were burned in a bonfire—with furniture, paintings, phonograph records, photographs, letters and unfinished stories—in the backyard of the house at 910 North Madison Street in Bloomington, Illinois, when an earlier life was coming to its end. Well, sitting in my room in the villa in Florence, I was reminded of sitting in the room in Ciudad del Maiz sixteen years before, and I thought again of how, lacking a dog with ticks, I got started. So, in Florence I rolled a sheet of paper into the typewriter and without any phrase or sentence or word as a cue for what might be written, I simply started to type. The third word that appeared on the page was the word "jelly" and as I remember I typed through it as quickly as I'd typed the two words before it and the thousands of words that followed. The word "jelly" however took on some peculiar significance, not especially in the fifteen and a half pages that were typed that night, but in what followed from those pages and that occupied me almost completely for the next six weeks.

Now, living in London for a while, I am writing this out not only for the autistic pleasure of resavoring that adventure, but also because I am interested in how that quite artificial beginning proved to be a back door that gave to a vista of past experience proved, once it was written and after some time had passed—a kind of enigma to me. So, in London I wrote out a kind of record of backtracking through the sequestered woods where I found what I'd already known: that my poem, "Jelly Was the Word" had sprung from the power of concrete experience and its predilection for transformation in memory. And, as became evident, much of the poem derives from quite specific, personal, even religious experiences.

But I do not want to get ahead of myself. We were talking about the evening of January 13th, 1962 in Florence and a kind of aimless continuous typing I did. These pages still hold some kind of interest for me, even though their real value lies not in themselves, but in what they got started going. The interest they hold is that old kind engendered by the curious and the absurd—bases for both fear and laughter.

At this point let it be known that I fully appreciate that the inclusion of these pages of non-sensical stuff could cause a serious interruption in the reading of this essay as a whole. Still, I must risk this since I feel it essential that prospective readers vicariously experience these pages of words even as they induced in me a comparable interruption in my regular life.

So, with only typographic errors corrected, the fifteen and a half pages follow:

A little jelly the man said, just as clearly as kittens are, and then he jumped in the elevator. The wheels and springs and seasons of our lives was the way he would have put, but cats aren't dogs and he knew it. After Friday, when the team was already in the infield moving out, he grasped at the second to the last straw and picked his teeth. That was before the argument about hard and he knew it. After Friday, when the team was already in the infield moving out, he grasped at the second to the last straw and picked his teeth. That was before the argument about hard versus soft money and easy street was just around the corner, some thought. But the drought hit hard and people, too, and the Cross of Gold speech was notable for its tarnishing.

Right after that the two-inch cuff came in vogue with rolled seams and butter almost a dollar a pound. End-of-track was within sight and the boomtown was a thing of the precisely past. Truck gardens were waiting to be invented with trucks while gardens were still. The subway under the Hudson was all but unknown except in Egypt, perhaps, but no one knew. The wind blew even without the tunnel and elevators were a thing still coming up, so far as the common man or common law was concerned. Then is when he said jelly in that way that condemned the present to some kind of future for which it waited almost in vain. But vain he was not, as he said jelly so well you could taste it, and even without bread or a pot in which to pitch it. Jelly, he said and set up the apple cart, right where a business college should have been. In the long run, if it has to be, there's always hope and faith in charity and that's what he preferred. Jelly is where the heart is and the heart is not where you hang your hat because that's not home not even, necessarily, a rack. Jelly, he said, just as clearly as you could hear a raindrop spread on the bed or cloth on the table.

But before he had a chance to have his comment jell into what it had been before the Whigs were reborn and Woodrow Wilson the Last was hung in a black frame, he died. Upon dying he took some kind of last in an unctuous way and then jelled. Turning into what you're saying is a fear for liars and not honest men, and he expressed that in Philadelphia before the post came out. Jelly he had said, and jelly he did, amen and glory to the potholder, woven or straw around the pot that's hot. And woe be to him who's cold.

But Jelly-saying man and his wife, of course, had a jelly son who was fluid. And when the sun came out clear as Greek mythology and everybody stood with baited lines, this son took hold of where his father had slipped and said in a voice reminiscent of his pater: jelly. Upon hearing this and all the sounds about mixed in as a kind of chorus without an anvil or even a tongs, the people kidnapped a child in effigy and tried to hear more. The son now on his own through notoriety and a sense of the uncommon in the generative found a small one-sided one and tried his best. But in the middle it broke and again there were two sides to everything. June was the month selected for the coming of July and the last week even of June. When it came there was a kind of calm and the word jelly was nowhere to be heard or found. Then as in all such cases that have hardened there came a softening. It was noticeable first at the edges and then in a little in from the foul line, but it was clear all the way through and through like unpitted glass or a bullet hole in the evening edition. This softening, like hardening in reverse with a public relations executive as an escort drove for home in a way that made you sick for the target. After leaving for Detroit in a southbound cab he found the meter running over and called for a cork. Once in Cork he found the Irish in an organization and not the least interested in the word, jelly.

There in Cork, like a bottle around, he did say it again and up came the half that was lost earlier and hardly found except for the end that doesn't count. Being alone and feeling rather depressed he defied. And then he sued for defecation of character in a court of the uncommon law where all the judges were benched and the ring was clear for the flyweights who were stuck on a girl from Somerset in the valley just under weight.

Yelling Jelly into the wind he rode the rods to Cincinnati and the long bridge that goes without a river to the far end of time on a clock in a tower that was built with stolen money and a lot of hard arms and on little cheese hods split up the middle. Not discouraged in the least, nor wishing for anything but a fair shot at the shoot, he depressed his aims to

give to the better. But Jelly was what he would say and after the teeth
were put back in and the law was blue-bonneted again, he said Jelly in a
way that jarred the rest of the mannerists left at New York University.
They took it to the Civil Liberties and had a kind of Passover with a net
below in case anyone fell or there was a serious discharge. Not wanting
to decrease the power of his own drive the son of Jellyman left that whole
situation to its own iconography and went where the acoustics were
good. That was in a small room in Victoria, Texas where the sheepmen
trade sheep and spit hard at a soft spittoon of gold and often hit. There
in that room before the bell rang and the sheep in clothing came in he
said it again. But the acoustics were so good and so self-contained—like
an ambassador from Peru or some other such country, if such there be,
suffering from creeping integrity—that he got a kind of regenerative
feedback through the shins. He was there in the Victoria room when she
came in with those veils and a glue for sticking letters to stamps.
Suffering as he was he still could smell, and he did. But she felt otherwise
and quite without a nose for self-protection, she batted the bird to a quiet
corner and squatted and then left it all for him. The vision of this, and a
little of that goes a long way, he took it on half fare because of his vertigo and his veterans status. Then, after the meat hook got loaded and
there didn't appear to be much more to say about the whole matter, not
even an anecdote or postscript, he wrapped it up in a piece of wax paper
neatly. This was out of character since he was. And feeling this he went
to a second-story window overlooking the under side and threw it out of
joint. Then coming back in earnest he jabbed at the cornball in the air
conditioner and felt better as the fan turned and time went ripping
through like ribbons in a shellfish. Then, recovered, he said it with all the
consonants—Jelly.

The papers came out in the evening and at the seams right on time
and he was there to read the sports section and union trade mark looking like a flaw in the rolled crystal glass. There it was as big as life and half
as strong and he knew it for what it was, Jelly. But the thing about it was
that he was the only one who knew and what he knew he knew he knew
new. So he folded it back into the parachute bag and stuffed a message

7

therein. Years later when the surplus parachute killed a good looking fellow over Burma when he was just under twenty the message came down to the Army and Navy store on the middle of what used to be Grover Cleveland's instep. The thing that got all those who knew was that the fuss raised was inadequate considering how things were, and the stakes involved. But came down it did right there from the air, true as the crow flies when shot. That part of the message then was lost, lost like a stone out of a kidney ring under proper care and very little cutting if you catch it in time, which he did. So feeling reimbursed for the loss and covered for the gains likely to be made by others he lofted his eyes to other spots on the wall. There he saw clear as da Vinci, we're told, and took it for what it was, but not without being underwritten. First he rubbed it a little and it smeared some. Then he patted it and it was tacky. Then he peeked at it when it wasn't looking just in case there was a ruse built in like a folding collapse or a cigar-lighter sponge. And he was right as his father might have told him: it was truly and only Jelly. He wiped all of it off and then took a little in a cup that had a plastic coat of arms where the lip should be and asked of it one simple question: are or are you not? There was no reply since it was. And then he said it again, out of a sort of door window that led to the dumb waiter who used sign language up a rectangular shaft that was full of draft beer, but only if there were cases in question. What came back was a kind of little Sir Echo in tights. But he was not averse to having the squeeze put on so he replied in kind. From that there were no results since an echo is an echo unless it's echolalia which he knew from the start was a bland form of insanity, barely recognizable in a crowd. However, the thing he was perhaps most wanting to avoid was cause for anyone from the other side to gain a wedge-hold on the thing he had to protect and, if possible, disseminate. So he held tight. As he squeezed it came out but not in a bunch, but rather in a kind of bloom like you fail to see in the dark areas of any good painting in the Uffizi or even, since they have an acquisitions fund, the Cleveland Museum. So as it got out in this squeeze he watched it go. It was a tailor-made kind of exit between his fingers leaving hardly a trace. Later, on a Leica negative found after the scourge that followed, you could see it but only in two dimensions. But there it was and clearly too: jelly.

Quietly and with the deftness of an empanelled Gordian knot he lettered out a sign in Old English with a crow-quill attached to a yolk sack. Then as quietly as he came, he left. The first man to see the sign couldn't read and the first man that could read was blind so there was a kind of open cockpit here without a plane or pilot, all unbottled gas in that particular shape. It was days before the sign was passed again, and with some pain because of its edges and corners coming around as they were in that now older English. And right after that there was a kind of solemn drawl that worked its way in a little deeper than was expected even by the informed. Then, just before the toast burned on the southern hemisphere near the larder, there came a boy from the hinterland who whistled as he worked. He could neither read nor write except Old English and Old Dog Tray. When he looked at the sign it was clear to him and he ran lickety-split over the marsh to the dike and stuck his finger in around the other fellow who was really doing the work since his finger was in the hole that matters. Knowing that it didn't wholly matter to him or the one in the wooden shoes, he gasped out, above the sound of following floods that he had read the word and the word was JELLY. The one in the wooden shoes and legs up to the hips there to be continued later in another joint, said he didn't believe a thing the other side was saying and at that the dam broke and the one who knew from the Old English was washed away like a sin in the flood.

In that way the sign was read and lost like long underwear in Tacloban where the rot comes up every day in the week and the strong. The trouble was, as we who are safe know, that it was written in the wrong language; it should have been written in Garlic or Handstand. The good thing about the tragedy is that it made success all the more imperative and when a thing is imperative it seldom spoils. This is what the son of the first Jellyman knew and this was his secret, which he wanted to undo. And there he was alive in Genoa where Columbus was long ago chewing like us and all the rest that we do and don't make much of. There he was on the pier with a sample in his pocket and a song on his lips, just jelly. The first man who came along was an American investor in a two-piece suit all in his face. The word was said as easy as a sneeze or a sneaked one under the table with a long cloth. The American investor acted as if he hadn't heard, which may have been true since his ears. Then he walked away as if he'd eaten and had his cake but with a suggestion of disbelief. At the end of the pier where the end gets to be the side and the water is near, he disappeared after something that looked strangely like his reflection in a kind of rubber raft with a spinnaker right after the bankruptcy one. Once the jelly man's son went over the hill to the rich. Lazarus had been there a few hours before, or so it seemed to the man in charge and he might have chalked the wall for a friend, but he didn't. He balked at chalking and that's where the hitch came at which our jelly man's sign tied up. He gave the word as if it were the most common and insignificant, like justice or fair play or honor, and no one heard even though there were thousands in the street hired not to hear him which should have made them listen with a menace.

A child playing with a plastic tongue blade and a reconstituted Boston pencil sharpener did look up in some kind of recognition of what this all meant in the street at that time like a sewer cover blowing off or putting bananas in the blowhole like they did in the Third Ward while Bobby Jones acted like this didn't matter. The child, upon this partial recognition of the stature of the presence, was hauled into a small kind of coop near the intake and to our knowledge was never seen again. One other flicker of recognition did, and that was in the opal eyes of a girl adjudged mad by a kind of pick-up band acting as a kangaroo court without a barrel one night when things were dull and all the playing cards were stuck together with brine and some kind of fish oil that was used for punishment. This girl heard the word and something in her came out big and not strong enough, however. What she did was rasp. Then she tried something even she would not have tried had she not heard: she gave her last schnecken to the one who liked schnecken more than anything else. This ultimate act of giving unto forbearance by your brother's keeper should have been recognized for what it was: a sign of knowing that it was jelly. But having discredited this girl's judgment, mind and body along with her future and past like deans do when it looks like there might be an idea in the college, no one, not even a mouse turned an edge or an ear her way. Having been rocked by the knowing of what was the highest, and not being able to share, she was left a little left of crippled and then withered off toward a stump standing in petrifaction by the second-hand white-colored Chevrolet with the rumble seat rumbling to itself but to no one else. She was never heard from again.

Years pass and the calendars come and go like pimples and gas on the stomach. Time is one thing, space is another and the hyphen isn't enough to fool. All time is a bundle unwrapping while the store is shut for the season and the stock is low by the marshes. It runs like a nose in the dark on someone you don't like. It pushes clocks around and stopwatches and prayer wheels in the shape of panama hats and gluts into your oil burner. Time is a thing without a handle or a spout, a kettle without fish, a back without a front, a beer without hops in the Scotch by the best place you can think of outside West Allis, Wisconsin. But any one you might ask would be pleased to tell you that time is a thing when, really, it's too late for having more than a short business meeting before the man from Kresge's tells the group how it is in the basement where it's all piled up and inventory on every legal holiday without pay working in the heat. And as this time, separated from space at the same cutting of the light from the darkness was going on, runs one man with the word was abroad with it in his mouth and on his tongue and shouting in the streets and on the corners in the valleys and over the hills down narrow-gauge speaking tubes and into open wounds and sewed up footballs so real they attracted pigs right down the lacings. The word was abroad in the way of the son of the original Jellyman and no one had ears to hear nor eyes that might try, or noses that should be paid more attention to with all the stink about.

The old adage has it that you, nor anyone else or his nephew, can keep a good man down. And Jelly-man was no exception. He went to the least expectant place he could imagine with his diver's helmet on and his ears stopped up. He went directly there in disguise in case he was misinformed as to who he wasn't. Once there he let it out again and people handed him bread, which is a beginning, but an end which is a heel. Clearly in this most unlikely place which was a church, he said jelly right among the prayers and Latin and music and again when the old women came in to work off their sins with the mops. This was a place the son of Jellyman always remembered because everybody smiled using their whole face way past the hairline—back and front in the case of beards. They were so gentle they had him almost painlessly garbled in a bag that was complicated with a germ of self-conceit. But all he had to do was walk a step or two out in the air of the street, out from under those Goldwater Gothic arches and stained gold frames to feel holy or whoever was near and more alive than that stuffed cornhusk man dangling in the Bridgewater, Massachusetts cavity near the door. Once in the air the solids get negative, by comparison at least, and that's what happened. Jellyman knew now that to go is where you think you shouldn't and there do what you must. Off he went like a man reading Freud backwards which is the correct way backwards to the old master himself. Off he went like a fully-cocked gun and a sprung lifer on a gift of freedom from the lame duck senate in the home state. This time he picked his way to an abortion clinic going full blast in the middle of the night. He came by the garden side over the razor blades and zip gun holsters around to the delivery room with a light burning in neon and all kinds of modern gas and bags and small incised notes that looked like hairlines on billiard balloons. The moon was high over the barbed wire at the back and a spade goat was on watch by the air compressor fitted with a brand name in red. The dew was thick on the executive board where it turns the edge toward self-service with no extra charge. He walked around the clapping boards to the cellar door used for dispatch and ingress where the sign said no people allowed unless at all costs, more by the yard, but who'll take it. There was no question mark; it just splayed out into the universe like an exploding dragonfly with bother in his bowels, or like that boy from Omaha when the Zero hit him in the punch press and he dog-hammered to nothing. Then there was the front door painted like it was in back, but with no gripping knobs or handles or hinges, just a kind of slab with screws around the edges and a sign that said welcome and through these doors pass the unborn who'll go the same, and the whole hog to boot and saddle one for the road. The light over the door was opaque black with dirt, and it was turned on full power at sixty cycles, the standard for the area. The steps had been removed, if he'd known, on the same Friday that Mary Miles Minter changed her name to Dolly Madison and tried to save the nation in the name of the dying President, and then went into good works, believing that anything is that does. The porch railing could hardly be heard it was so soft to the touch, and it ran right across the Egyptian-type false door. Then he went to the northeast corner of the clinic where the screams were muffled in the angle and where the clapboards applauded in that fancy way. There never had been a door here, and there wouldn't be one as long as he waited or hired some mercenary from one of the new nations to wait forever for him. Knowing this, he rapped on the corner of the clinic as the work inside went on to the music of a Hammond eggs organ. The soprano singing under the rose-tinted bulb near where Doctor Leghorn was pulling and swabbing at his trade, heard the knocking as if in a dream tightly bundled and bound. But she doubted that a knocking could come at a corner or that anyone would knock such a good square thing. Jellyman's son was encouraged by the absence of reception and felt in his heart of hearts and spades that here he might be heard once he would shock them out of the unexpectancy. So he knocked again with the handle of his bronze umbrella he'd assumed after losing his father so early in life. And then it happened.

The burglar alarms went off and the roof opened up and Doctor Leghorn left in a helicopter with all the evidence in tow with the last cable tripping a capstan that fell over on a dynamite cap that got a landmine going and blew off the whole clinic, babies, buntings and awls. For a while it rained junk as steep as the side of the Chinese Wall and piled on the ground like suggestions for improving the race. After a little smoke and dust full of rust and other colored oxides, the ceramic fixtures came down almost intact. Standing mute as if he held a piece of marlin spike seamanship by the numbers, the son of Jellyman stood somewhat longer and watched with the patience of a piece of schist wrapped in the protection of Pele's hair. The garden of abortive junk bloomed into the sign of a ratchet with the drop-piece in place between the teeth, and then materialized on the ground near the circumcised water main. In the quiet of this double-feature aftermath, the son of Jellyman leaned close. He brought his elbows up for inhaling and into the teeth of the ratchet shining there, he spoke the word with the clarity of a revenue man: jelly. The ratchet lay there without effect, diameter, circumference, radius, teeth and all, and made no response while the rumble of the echoes of the raining junk came back from the cloisters belonging to the main concentration camp called the Metropolitan Museum by the wordy and the crypt by the cryptic. Jellyman the second, son of the first and maybe the last, cried aloud and with maximum voiced the word while the junk kept at its assignment to rust.

But everyman knows that the dawn is darkest before the night and the evening feast is better than any breaking of fast, and Jellyman had an identification with his father and that brought him close to everyman. Waiting, then, like for a train in Alberti's Sant Andrea, under the crossing where the information booth should be and far ahead of the pinball panel altar, and wondering who of the men of cloth and a yard wide had the ball in monstrance of the fact, Jellyman rolled a target on a rubber belt machine that should be in the Smithsonian right under the Spirit of St. Louis, leather jacket and all. Not without some estimate of the quality of this nonchalance in the face of fervor for neglect, Jellyman tried breathing with alternate lungs to gain a perspective by incongruity. The wax ball thus produced, gave to a slow melt and the drippings were scavenged by the anti-guano league that worked in silence behind the cardboard sign that read from the back. With his shoes growing thin under the burden of his own unheard word, and the organs of his voice box strained in the formation of Jelly, the son of Jellyman approached the hiatus between answer and question, halfway to the unsanctified pantry full of waiting bread. Holding his hand on the throttled answer and with steam from boiler number one sneak-previewing the end unsought, he came down the grade to a jump into crescendo as clear as Sun Valley full of Swedes in skis and not in jeopardy, piled up his breath like frozen foods in the downtown supermarket and then let go. It came out clear as crystal gazing ahead, but its sound lay in the valley like that of a bell made of meat. Someplace there may have been rejoicing, like in Mailer or Miller on the floss, but it was no place close like Muddville where, struck, Casey swung out. Here at the fringe of the hard-bought junk where the urinals and bidets stood and the ratched lay unhorsed, there was no rejoicing, no reification, no plus or minus round or square to the roots or hell and gone. It was, rather, a special kind of nothing, the kind saved up for burials, gas-powered ouija boards, thumbnail oil paintings in mud, morticians' manuals, extinct junco birds and the space between the joists. It was a refined nothing not unlike the uninvented zero to the googol power with the same left over, undecorated and unsung and no moaning as it crossed the bar in a Maya glyph. And as the nothing it surely was in any language learned or forgotten in the subway or penthouse, school or in bed, faded into the usual something, Jellyman was encouraged as he remembered that in mathematics and the good you carry the zero. So stuffing it into a Dunn and Bradstreet knapsack lying there in the silently wrangling junk, he slung it over his shoulder in the clover while time was decaying in the hay nonny. Then, feigning departure like a false unconstipation rectified only to return, he took a step forward and held it like the one not in the bush. No thing moved and there was no sound in the glut on knees bent and twisted in that pile driving silence deeper than the magnet that makes all compasses go north before berserk. Unflagged, Jellyman, son of Jellyman gone, trained his way through the red block beyond end-of-track and walked to the edge of the silhouette cut from junk. But still, there could be no sound. And into this he called the word, fleshed it out incarnate with his own never worn on his sleeve nor made much of like intellect or a larger organ played by the Baptists in lieu of a wine-drinking god. Into this he called the word and instead of going it came and stuck like a bone of fish in the palette on the floor below the roof of his mouth.

Defeat is kind meat and just to those whose victory is in that, and each defection of the other's ears is power to the other's tongue. But it was getting dark now around the rim where everybody before Magellan fell off in a hammer-head stall, and Jellyman knew it was after time to eat.

And when it was black all around and those who might be living would be going to sleep, he stayed awake by virtue of that. Opportunity knocks but once, unlike in drowning where there's two chances before the pay-off with the music and the green going down and all the sins and caviar go up so happily in wet smoke. The light of the world was not extinguished by Burne-Jones or the handgun with the algebraic proclivity for equalization. In full knowledge and regalia of such absolute facts, Jellyman watched through the night and listened into tomorrow for the opportunity and the light, calling with every other breath—so there'd be room for the response—the word; and the word was Jelly in every language of everything and everybody. Over the fornicating junk it went to the woods on the periphery and over the sides to drip its consonants and vowels all night as the dawn came up like mush from Quaker's across the breakfast table. Exhausted but not dismayed and with a hardening of purpose reserved for arteries in others, Jellyman girded. He trussed up his voice on spindles colloidal and got the checkerboard muscles good and taut above his belt in the plexus reserved for the sun. Like a harp full of orchestras in moving vans playing all the way across Kansas and drowning out the Cincinnati hit parade, he keyed himself more for the final shout on this location. He mustered the hollows for resounding, stiffened the bosses for the strike, arched his back double down as far as Moses and came out the other side. He filled the cavities of his lungs with air stacked under pressure back of his esophagus, and burst it forth in a blast, the one word, Jelly.

From a primordial dung heap under the junk a pale Alaskan husky emerged to look and then to bark and bite at the knapsack stuffed with the zero clear up to the leather straps. He showed his paws without any thorns, then strengthened by the fill of strap he bounded from whence he'd come, feet, tail, ears and all, back to the compost without a bugle blowing. Jellyman, taken by any sign of life looked down at his shoes where the Duco held the bows in place, saddened by this husky disappearance. From a crack no bigger than a hairsplit on the ground between his feet he saw a thread of blue smoke coming out in the shape of a celluloid French curve, and he watched it rise and turn into a balloonist, second class, a little to the right and some west of where the husky started down. He yelled Jelly to the balloonist, and some must have gotten to the balloon, too, but the balloonist was bagging his sand for a drop and his ears were all rings and no drum. Who knows who's testing who in times like this, and who knows what balloonist may have the key or even just a wee bolt to nut the lock. And as he faded in the limiting Renaissance perspective, there above the hardware remains of the abortion clinic, Jellyman intoned the word straight along to the vanishing point and so it did. There in the hole where the point goes through to the Oriental learning by rote with a brush on an empty stomach lined with tradition and bearded sandals in philosophical stripes, Jellyman saw his word slip through and get swallowed up. Patience is the guide through the forest as any ranger knows from his tower even if not equipped with a phone, and patience was what Jellyman had to pair off with the word. For a while he waited as if there might be a train or a verdict or someone coming back for an adjustment or appeal, but he waited alone while a desiccated rubberband on a south Cuban beach waited too, only in the sun unknowing. Patience like mercy is often strained and grated and ground and rolled out in patties for poultices for the stomach but not for the soul. Strained, patience is a heller at the bit, no matter how much free verse tries to pass as poetry with guarantees in the preface. And strained it breaks wind and the clay pigeon but not the real, and Jellyman was real. With bent but not lost patience then, he got down and fell, but only asleep, and only until the unity of one was collected like scum from the water's edge of his consciousness. The moon struck pay dirt about four and Jellyman was on his way again.

He found a path some pathfinder had lost and blazed a trail crosswise to a seminary midway between Atlanta and the sea on his way from the ridiculous to the supine. Taking a cue from the voile dress salesman he'd known in the Dakotas where the road goes flat from Cottonwood to Wasta, he was not averse to unscheduled stops in search of a sale or just goodwill for the plant back home. And there stood the seminary in solid brick with a belfry and true arches facing the arroyo. The dean was at a board meeting and the seminarians were getting enough Greek to get a long little dogie tight in the manger with lice that they hoped would lend an air of dedication. At the monument to Hebrew in the plastic covered atrium just inside the outside walls a gaunt lad from New Dime Box, Texas picked at his Christology for an exam at noon. His books were in a green bag on his back like a Camelite hump and they counterbalanced his open necktie and regular fellow attitude. He had his seams rolled under his hat where his forehead buttoned down to the job at hand, under the abridged Rosary bookmark that dangled a beer opener. The back of his head was reflected in the pool table where his better-prepared mates took their cues and pees. The halls were decked with Medici balls in honor of prosperous Christian Humanism and the historically frank stare at the after image of the unity of one. Over the scene that was quietly suggestive of a brick and glass anagram built out of last words of traffic victims, there hung a cloud of false witnesses bearing tidings for the new curriculum.

Jellyman taking in the scene, aimed his steps for the soft white underside of the young seminarians' collective unconscious. Striking a pose like the Gattamelata on a cross horse, and raising himself by the straps of his own molasses he gargled some spare saliva quite out loud. And when the seminarian heard, which was pronto but muffled a little, he jumped to his knees stabbing himself with his Zippo aflame and cried into a gauze receptacle that came with his textbooks. Now was the chance to be heard if ever it was and Jellyman pronounced the word Jelly. The seminarian turned back into what he was before and in the same position along the edge of the monument to Hebrew, only to underline a phrase in the book: when in doubt ride the Creed Steed. Jellyman yelled the word into his ear and the seminarian was stone deafness in tweed and a little cold lard higher up around the hair looking up and down footnotes for the noon examination.

Jellyman, just about convinced that he was in the wrong place to try to have the word heard, still persisted around the fountain of the seminary to the chapel where a large group of the conservative branch from outside Scranton was going through the Sunday plays diagrammed in penicillin on the washstand where holy water was no longer allowed. He poked his head through one of the open jalousies near the stainless steel image of working together for more and more of the same right near the boyhood seminarian who didn't notice because he was trying to memorize with his eyes shut. A 45-rpm machine was making the music through a mock-up pipe organ facade ingeniously contrived by the last graduating class from Japanese war surplus material then being sold on the open market on dark days. The music was from other records transcribed with the surface noise boosted to the fore, thereby allowing the nationality of the composer to be disguised. It was slow, though, even in the tweeter nailed to the crosswalk under the polyethylene vault. The seminarians were wearing waterwings filled with melted macadam on their feet in order to trace their movement around the mensa and thereby make a graphic record of how they'd done for purposes of the closed critique to follow. Jellyman took a place, then, at the door near the Tarvia machine and the common prayer dispenser and waited for some kind of opening. It came when the wax mannequin of the bishop listed candelwise and caught on fire. Quickly it fell bending on the floor and heaped high in flames, sport section and all. The running wax in flames ignited the melted macadam from the wings of the seminarians, still strapped and bound to their feet, and the massive hotfoot was a reality in more than Christian principle. The seminarians—there must have been close to a battalion—pogo-sticked their way toward the locked door of the investment room. Then, as the exvested, seminarians fumed in their own pews and ran wild in the chapel, Jellyman came through the jalousie and mounted the gunny sack flag over the mensa to call out his word. He called it out loud and colloidal and the fire died and the bishop's mannequin unmelted back into the form it was and all was as before. And in the relative silence he called out the word again and no one heard as they skated again on the waterwings, filled with cool macadam right past the chart in penicillin by the washstand. Having had almost no hope from the beginning in this place of unstuffed reliquaries, Jellyman came down from the gunnysack flag and left the grounds in the other direction.

On the ridge named pole by a Russian some years before the invention of spectacles disguised as hearing aids, Jellyman turned back for one last sentimental look at the seminary now looking like that Civil War photograph of Atlanta, and sighed as the wind in the pruned trees soughed. A biplane with six pitot tubes flew over trailing a sign in the sky saying Social Security is Love in our Own Time.

Over the ridge where the path falls down, Jellyman saw Camp Pinkerton named after the major who protects things in glove cases and is rumored catches thieves at the battery terminals. The pup tents were neat in rows between the crosses row on row your own boat oh gently down the scream, and the officers' mansions were covered with hors d'oeuvres and new model flags with gilded balls and nylon lines aflapping smartly in the backdraft of another comic investigation still pending on grounds of brutality to the literate while on duty under the toilet articles of war. It looked like something no one would paint any color, especially not where the motor pool was with half-track bicycles, four-wheel drive hand grenades, pestle shooting mortars, rockets in the shapes of ambulances and congressional medals of honor, tanks with anthologies painted on the side facing La Spezia where Shelley took too much water, amphibious bazookas in baby carriages and Trafalgar Square trucks with transistor transmitter-receivers in the rear end all lined up so neat you could hear a pin prick. The grounds were policed clean of all spit and polish with the help of a group of integrated draftees and volunteers from every state in the union plus spies from abroad. The motto of the camp, though informally posted on the watertower was fading now in the same dust that was making the sunset so Ektachrome: The Only Good Hero is a Dead Hero. It was signed Anonymous in fish bait by a Private from New Orleans.

With that mention of a soldier from New Orleans I stopped typing, not because the flow of words had lessened but because my fingers could no longer work the keys. From the beginning to the end I had typed as fast as I could in order to allay the possibility of reflecting upon what I was saying through the machine.

And after I quit, I lighted up a cigar and read it over slowly. None of it engaged me with anything propositional, metaphysical or even philosophical, though I couldn't miss the skewed but recurrent references that implied events from the Christian legend. Mainly it made me laugh. It sounded curious, macabre, but also real and true in some way. It was both funny and frightening: the way language seemed to turn back on itself, take revenge on propositional logic as it ricocheted from nonsense to pseudo-sense, from echo to first sound and back and across without loss of energy. I patched up some places where the keys had stuck and caused letters to pile up on themselves, and then I went to bed.

In the morning I could hardly wait to see these pages again, and after reading them to the first sounds of motor scooters in the street below, I wondered why it was that the word "jelly" became so important throughout the thing. After all, this was the word, and the only word, put into the mouth of the almost bodiless protagonist, and because he kept mouthing it, he was called "Jellyman," just as his father for whom it was the total vocabulary, was called "Jellyman the First." It's true that long ago, when I was a kid, we recited that rhyme about Santa Claus who had a belly that shook like a bowl full of jelly. And it's true also that later we sang a song that had something to do with "it must be jelly 'cause jam don't shake so much," or was it the other way around? And I always remembered—and still do, with undiminishing clarity—the fistfight I had with my older brother in the basement of the house where we were staying back in the spring of 1930. We rocked each other from one space to another and wound up in the fruit cellar throwing jars of apple butter and jelly at each other. They smashed against the walls and splattered across the ceiling and over the floor, and we ended up a single jellied mess. And still later, of course, we knew about vaginal jellies and all the jokes that went with that—from giving birth to jelly beans to putting up pubic preserves. But, as I sat there that morning after breakfast in Florence, thinking about what I'd written and about jelly, my mind kept running a background scene full of planets and stars. I went to the *Oxford Universal Dictionary* that I'd packed across the ocean with me, and under the word jelly, 2b, I read this: "Applied to the alga *Nostoc*, which appears as a jelly-like mass on dry soil after rain and was supposed to be the remains of a fallen star." Then down below there's a quotation from someone whose name is given as Somerville—"Like that falling Meteor, there she lies, a Jelly cold on earth." Now I don't know if I ever really knew, in these specific terms, that jelly had this connotation, but I do know that on reading this in the dictionary a series of similar feelings for the word were reactivated. And I do recall an uncommon pleasure, actually an excitement, in equating the characteristically colloidal quality of organic life with fallen and metamorphosed stars. And if one were to have just one word that he was given to shout about on the earth, then maybe jelly would not be the poorest choice: it's the name of our substance, our being.

With that somewhat settled in my mind, I read over and over again those fifteen and a half pages. It was clear that what they carried was a kind of ambiguous, involuted, pun-packed progress report that got nowhere in particular. It mainly concerns a peregrine character, *Jellyman*, in a variety of places and grotesque situations in which the bizarre, the ludicrous and the incongruous seem to be taken for granted. Into this shifting grotesquery Jellyman calls out his word with little or no effect. Not so strange, really, and beguiling, I thought. I left my room, took a walk up the Via Montughi to the old Bologna road, only to know again that the awful Florentine winter was still running its course, and then jogged back to my room. Effortlessly at first, it seemed, I began to write from the material of those first fifteen pages as if what I was doing was immensely important. For the next six weeks, which ran past the middle of February, a quality of purposeful engagement strung the hours and the days together. On Sunday, the 18th of February, I finished a thing, a poem which I later called by that persistent word, jelly: "Jelly Was the Word."

Now the reason for writing this book is not to tell the story of the poem or even what it might mean. The story is simple enough; much of it derives directly from those first fifteen pages, and much more from the clues they held out to me. It has to do with this curious character who has some kind of obsession or mission to speak and to yell and to bray and whinny and whisper and shout that one word, jelly. And that is what he does in places like New York University; downtown Cleveland, Ohio; Tillamook Bay, Oregon; a bank in Victoria, Texas; Denver; Soldier Field in Chicago; an automobile graveyard outside Los Angeles; and other places across the country. Almost without exception, the word is not heard or the responses to it are in some way mistaken, false or only partial. At the very end of the poem the word becomes unutterable in the presence of its incarnate meaning. This happens in St. Louis, Missouri in the backroom studio of an artist who keeps on painting as Jellyman, dumbstruck and in fits on the floor, loses the word "like the ghost." I feel pretty safe in saying that the poem I wrote is about the artist as hero; but as I said, it is not my purpose, here, to try to describe its pattern or tell its meaning.

Once the poem was complete, I knew how it was, and that, for me, it was over and done with. And once it was complete and its signs and clues lay there on the table before me, I became interested in something else: what lay back of what had been written. It is true, of course, that those pages of what could be called automatic writing and which provided a fabric of words, images, actions and ideas from which to begin— those pages lay back of the poem in a most significant and perhaps obvious way. However, specific and detailed personal experiences also lay back of even the most curious and bizarre passages of the poem. These experiences had been generalized and transformed in the process of writing

Donald Weismann

and, in fact, had become so convolved and imbedded in the fabric of the whole that upon reading the poem a week after it was finished, it took on a character so much its own that it was not easy to identify myself with what had often started as rather specific personal experiences. The fact of the matter is, as I've already said, that once the poem was finished and I went back to read it, it took on something of an enigmatic quality. Evidently this quality is undeniable in it. Some readers have commented not only upon its absurd quality but also upon its quality of engaging and persuasive perplexity. Still, the personal experiences that lay back of the poem had never seemed curious or enigmatic to me—neither while the actual experiences were unfolding, nor later when I was recalling and remembering them. Another possibility has always existed, however: maybe the writing of the poem had uncovered something whose existence I had previously not been entirely conscious of; namely, that the very experiences which lay at the root of many of the passages in the poem were, in and of themselves, absurd, comical, pathetic and outlandish but in such ways that only when they were strung together in the poem did these root characteristics become clear. And not only that: maybe the poem was showing me that, in fact, life is without the character or the meaning we assign it in our efforts to make it square with our childhood estimate of the conventions and institutions that provided us with the absolutes of good and evil, reason and madness, and that either prolonged our innocence or assured our ignorance.

So, perhaps for mainly personal reasons, I thought it might be rewarding to go back through the poem, locate clues to specific past experiences, and try to recall them or the climate of their happening. If I were to accomplish nothing else by doing this, still my efforts might intimate something about what happens to the traces of raw experience and to ourselves in the process of creating a new and self-sufficient coherency, no matter how curious, outlandish or ordinary.

The first stanza opens the door with the word that no one hears:

Jelly, he said, and no one got the word,
Not even gooseflesh in the backdraft.

And the "backdraft" here alludes not so much to the rush of air that
fills the vacuums created by the force of spoken words, as it alludes to the
tacit character of any event—even so simple an event as the sounding of
a single word. So, I mean to make point of the fact that not only is the
word not heard for the word it is, but more than that, its "backdraft," its
tacit character, the clues its sounding might be carrying are not enter-
tained by anyone: no one gets "gooseflesh in the backdraft." No one sens-
es in that "backdraft" that there exists clues to something of value or of
just plain interest to them. They do not respond, for instance, to the possibility that this word might carry clues to new, more inclusive tacit
knowledge of the world and of themselves. For myself, it seems I am reg-
ularly looking for such clues—for messages in bottles, as Walker Percy
has put it, that carry news from beyond the island on which I live. And
as a painter and maker of collages, such clues occur as often for me in the
auras of colors and objects as in the "backdrafts" of spoken words. I've
written about this in an essay called "The Collage as Model."

It all goes something like this. Beginning with an object of
particular visual and associational qualities, *and* with its power to
affect me at that very time with considerably more than ordinary
intensity, I begin to seek its context. Or, I could say that I begin

to seek for the ideal context in which this incomplete thing will appear completed. I move the object as I move in relation to it; I see it in a variety of visual environments, a continually running trial-and-error kind of seeking. After a while, in just enough cases, the object begins to ask for certain kinds of support for the color violet, for the metallic gray qualities of the daguerreotype, for lines that lose to a haze. I try other objects, bits, and pieces in the vicinity of the first. I paint and draw around some parts, modulate others with the cloudiness of overlaid x-ray photographs. I enhance and obliterate until something like a neighborhood of compatibles begins to assert itself. This assertion shifts, but at a stage it begins to limit these shifts through a much narrower range. Then a direction is sensed and followed with a finer care. I find myself tasting the colors as they come together, savoring them and rejecting, or savoring and saving, all within a more limited range than any time up to this. I have a sense of hefting the sizes and shapes, the pictorial weights; I physically feel the textures through my hands and my eyes, all the while any photographic or printed, drawn or painted images are adjusted for maximum effect. Then, ultimately, like the last split second before the forgotten name of someone moves from the tip of one's tongue to full recovery and clear articulation, I feel the impact of completion—the discovery or realization of a *coherency* existing among the formerly disparate and incomplete things. Each time it is arrived at, this coherency comes as a surprise even though it is that, precisely, toward which I must have been working. This end which is sought, this new coherency, unity, or radiance which does not actually exist for me until it comes into evidence at the end of the creative process, is yet present in some way throughout that whole process. From beginning to end, it haunts the voyage of discovery as an ambivalent allure, and it is that from which the searcher does his dead reckoning—or so I sense I do mine.

It is my hope that talking like this will help to flesh out some intentions of this first stanza of the poem, and also to alert the reader to how this larger work is likely to progress and eventually turn out.

The complete text of the poem, "Jelly Was the Word" is given in the Appendix herewith.

The second stanza consists of three lines.

Jelly was the word as surely as
A fair ball batted backwards
Is foul.

My father, who played a lot of baseball when he was a young man, achieved the height of his baseball career in those seasons he played third base for the Slocum Hatworks in Milwaukee. Long after he stopped playing, he attended baseball games and I suppose it was no accident that back around 1920 or '21, our family rented a house at 707 Chambers Street, directly behind home plate of what was then called the Milwaukee Brewers Baseball Park. Even though there was a ball-stopping screen up along the top of the grandstand, a lot of foul balls arched over it and landed in the street in front of our house or on our roof and, on more than one occasion, they came crashing through our bay window. And even though as a little kid of six or seven years old, I got in to see some complete baseball games at the Milwaukee Brewers ballpark, still, as a kid, the isolated phenomenon of the foul ball played a big place in my life. I suppose that if we had lived on the other end of the park—that is, out on the street behind left or right field, and could have hoped for homerun balls to come over the fence and in through the front window of our house over there—if that had been true, I suppose I'd have had a special fix on the home-run ball. But as it was our house was back of home plate and I developed a fix on the foul ball.

In those long ago days before radio and certainly before television, the way you got to witness a sports event was to attend the sports event, unless now and then you got to see some weeks-old spectacular plays in a Pathé Newsreel. In those days admission to see a professional baseball game came pretty high for our means. We didn't often attend baseball games though it was a fairly regular custom to let the kids in free of charge after the seventh inning. So when there was a ballgame going on on Sunday afternoon we very often sat on the front porch and, sitting there, we could just about visualize the game as it went along. We could hear the umpire calling strikes and balls and safe and out. We could hear the crack of the ball against the bat and we could hear the crowd stamp and roar. It was a simple matter of knowing what inning it was by keeping tab of the relatively quiet times between; and no game ever ended while we sat on our front porch with our being surprised at the fact that it was over. So, on Sunday afternoons, very often as I remember, at least a couple of us kids and my father and now and then my mother, would be sitting on the front porch of 707 Chambers Street hearing the baseball game. And every now and then the wonderful thing would happen: a foul ball would go up from the bat, up over the screen and come bounding toward our front porch. More than that, if we kept the street swept with our eyes, and if we were always ready to run, we could pick up other foul balls that were not aimed specifically at our house. In those days we had a lot of balls, all foul balls, lined up on a special shelf in the living room, a kind of reliquary, and there they stayed until I don't know when. Us kids didn't play with them because we were said to be too little, and the balls were big and hard or so they seemed, and my father's days of playing baseball had long been over. My father used to say that when a baseball pitcher took up the ball, he held in his hand a fair ball. All balls were fair, my father said, unless they were hit foul. I can remember that this pronouncement, which I'd heard more than once, he used as a kind of moral that he'd recite in special circumstances. I can remember that as I heard my father say this, I was a little troubled by the whole thing. I'd stare at one of those balls on shelf in the living room and think about how it had started out fair but then it became foul. And there it was, nothing more and nothing less than a foul ball on the shelf. I wondered whether some balls weren't really foul from the beginning and that this fact was proved when the batter hit it foul. Years later when I played third base on the Milwaukee County Home for Dependent Children's baseball team, and when I came up to bat, I often heard myself saying like a litany: don't throw me a foul, don't throw me a foul. Then, too—back there on Chambers Street—I thought that some balls had been created to be fair forever and that no batter, not even Zip Hauser, could hit them foul no matter how hard he tried. As a kid I knew something about fair balls but an awful lot more about foul balls.

It doesn't surprise me, then, that in the second stanza of my poem a role for the foul ball was found. More than that, I may have at last come to terms with my father's concept of balls, fair and foul. It seems, by what I say in these three lines, that I came to agree with my father since I didn't say merely that a ball batted backwards is foul; rather I said, a fair ball batted backwards is foul. Yes, my father was right: as the pitcher picks up the ball and the game is started, he starts with a fair ball. Yes, all balls start out being fair. It's only when they're batted backwards, back of home plate toward our house on Chambers Street, that they become foul and that's a sure fact. And that's what I wanted to say in this second stanza, that yes, Jelly was the word, just as surely as a fair ball batted backwards is foul.

In stanza three, where I call people by the clothes they wear in order to suggest a wide variety of types symbolic of people to whom the word Jelly was addressed—I allude to some people in double-breasted pinstripe suits and to some people robed in worms. The stanza reads like this:

The word was his to voice abroad
In hopes it could be heard by anyone
In certainty or doubt,
Dungarees or double-breasted pinstripes,
Robed in worms or cloth or naked
In wisdom or ignorance, stretching to marvel
The excarnation of the hooded false.

Long before I became familiar with the movie type developed to stand for all gangsters—the average height man with dark eyes and dark complexion, dressed in a broad-brimmed fedora and a double-breasted suit with widely spaced pinstripes—long before I became familiar with that type, long before I knew of a man by the name of Humphrey Bogart, double-breasted pinstripe suits stood for something very specific to me.

When my Uncle Charlie, who had been a machine-gunner with the Rainbow Division in France during World War I, came home to our house on Clybourne Street—after a year of "mowing 'em down like Kansas wheat," and after something like two years in the army of occupation—he took off his uniform in the living room, pants and all, and announced that from there on out it was going to be double-breasted pinstripes for him. My Uncle Charlie stayed with us for about two months and during that time he had his first double-breasted pinstripe suit made by a tailor with a high reputation. When the day came for my Uncle Charlie to go Out West, my father and I went down to the Union Station with him to say good-bye. My Uncle Charlie was wearing his new double-breasted pinstripe suit; and when the engine began to puff and blow and that whistle let go, he swung up the steps and into what seemed to me a car headed straight for the Promised Land.

It was three years later and I was in the fourth grade when my Uncle Charlie returned to Milwaukee for a visit. He'd made a lot of money Out West. My father said that he was a rich man—and he came back wearing a double-breasted pinstripe suit. The stripes were very white and the suit was very black all around the stripes. My Uncle Charlie stayed at our place for a couple of weeks, time enough for me to notice that after he'd unpacked and hung his things in the closet, there were four double-breasted pinstripe suits hanging there.

Since that day back in the twenties, fashion has had pinstripes and double-breasted suits come and go. But so far as I know, the feeling I have that such a suit is hard evidence of a decision to change life, to be some sort of dapper success in this world, dates back to two years after the first World War with my Uncle Charlie standing in the living room and announcing with absolute finality that for him, it would be double-breasted pinstripe suits from there on out. His reappearance some years later, dressed in such a suit and carrying four more in his orange leather bag, only served to reinforce this conviction in me. And I suppose that series of events with my Uncle Charlie is really what was responsible for my having tailor-made in Guadalajara after World War II, a very dark double-breasted pinstripe suit—totally out of fashion at the time—and I'm also presuming that it was this series of events, with my Uncle Charlie, that had me allude to people most likely to be dressed in double-breasted pinstripe suits: a stylish, dandyish, worldly kind of people who, if they hadn't made a real success, at least knew they'd made the decision and were making off as if they had.

Now the allusion to people robed in worms had its root in a much more specific and private experience. In my freshman year at college, a very small college of twelve hundred students, I carried a course of a general sort that came under the heading of Sociology in the college catalogue. It was required as most of the freshman courses were in those days and, strangely, still are. A Mrs. Giselda Slaughter taught the course. She was a manly woman of about forty-eight or fifty. All the students, it seemed, knew that she had been married and that she was divorced. That in itself was nothing special, not even back then. But more than that, they talked about Mrs. Slaughter as if they were privy to macabre details of her unsuccessful marriage and prolonged divorce proceedings. Having heard this sort of thing even before entering her class served to focus interest in her rather than in the course.

Now, my closest friend in those days was a fellow student named John J. Mimier, now a very successful tax expert with lots of men working under him in Dallas and about the state. In those days John was interested in drawing and painting and I thought that he was an excellent writer. To me, his drawings were about as fine as those of Michelangelo. The stories he wrote and read to me, or just told to me, always moved me. Even now I can recall two of them. One was called the "Saga of a Nickel" and over about twenty-five or thirty pages, it followed a five-cent piece through the hands of a lot of only disparately related people whose portraits John drew with an uncommonly revealing line. The other story was called "Mother" and it concerned the death of a woman, a mother, who had been insane for a long time. John told me that he had learned, in some kind of journal, of a disease usually associated with a specific form of insanity that caused the skin to leave the body. John made use of this in the story, and the final episode of the mother's death, with her face coming off in the pillow, was as grotesque as it was moving.

John and I sat next to each other in Mrs. Slaughter's Sociology class. Both of us, though at first taken by her nervous power, soon found ourselves thoroughly disliking, if not hating, her. By all standards I knew of then and know of now, Mrs. Slaughter was unfair. After ingratiating herself to us she would turn and abuse the trust she had engendered, all the while appearing remotely occupied with something beyond and totally unknown to us. She was caustic, mean, spoiling for destructive argument, and she perhaps was very sick. Before the course was half over, it had become a habit for John and I to take her bait and ask relevant but embarrassing questions in class, and though both he and I received A's on all tests she had given, still we received average grades for the course. There was something about Mrs. Slaughter that called up a profound pity in me. Even though she came to class beautifully dressed and perfectly made up, to me she seemed to be dying, and she knew it, and was fighting back by making signs that she still could affect the living for whom she had lost all love. I can remember watching her move like a mystery about the room, to the blackboard, back to her desk, and now and then to the window, as she talked, often it seemed, to herself. And I can remember feeling with something that felt like certainty, that she was being eaten alive from inside. It was one afternoon when I was thinking things like this that John, who was in the seat to my right, leaned over and in a very low voice said, "My God, I believe she's robed in worms." It sent a chill through me and as I looked at Mrs. Slaughter standing there at the front of the room, I saw her dark green dress as a fabric of worms, and felt them on myself.

Mrs. Slaughter left the faculty the following year and as far as I could imagine, she left to find some place to die. I have often wondered if I would have remembered Mrs. Slaughter as long as I have if John had not said those words, and with them epitomized the quality of presence that this woman had for me then and for all those years between—from the very early 1930s in Milwaukee to 1962 in that room in Florence where I found them again, and wrote them into the poem. In the poem they stand for the sick and the doomed, for those who know that the face has turned away from them. And that in contrast to those who wear double-breasted pinstripe suits, like my Uncle Charlie. But no matter if it was my Uncle Charlie or Mrs. Slaughter, or others in dungarees, plain cloth or naked, I meant to include them all, in their wisdom or ignorance, in pity or without pity, in grace or fallen from grace, stretching to marvel at the stripping away of every falsehood "the excarnation of the hooded false."

Through the years I've become acquainted with the devious ways in which thought moves, and then moves us. I know something about how unbid ideas—whole patterns of thought and action—stir in a view down a street or into a backyard, how the most complicated concept is often born in the aura of a simple hunch. I am not a stranger to the beguiling waywardness of what we still call the mind, nor to the gifts of knowing to which this way often points. And as one of those people who drew and painted whole worlds before writing a single sentence, I know that we always know more than we can say. There are just all sorts of things that will forever remain beyond saying. Some things we have to whistle or dance or walk or wrestle into reality. It is only some things that can find their reality in words. Still I wish it were possible for me to say more than I'm able to say about what lies back of one of the lines in stanza four of the poem, and, more particularly, just five words of that line.

In order to say what I might be able to say, it will help to bring out the whole stanza:

When the sun came out, stripped as Greek mythology in Basic
    Esperanto,
He formed the word full in the leeside air of a hill
Upstream so it would carry the load of tidings down
Almost according to the local weather prediction, and maybe
Get through to the most unsuspecting.
But those about were in mezzo-humanist chorus
With anvils, tongs and sledges
Beating out shoes for plaster casts of deep-freeze Parthenon horses

While singing to keep their ears pragmatically deaf.
He funneled the word down and lofted it on high,
But unhearing they went about their copyrighted schedule to noon
When they kidnapped a child in effigy, the daily ritual
For keeping the curriculum from jeopardy
And untowardness.

The five words in line twelve, are "kidnapped a child in effigy."

Now, in the course of my life I've read an awful lot of newspaper stories about kidnapping. Besides those political and absolutely insane ones that for a while went briskly along with the hijacking of airplanes, besides those, perhaps the most recent one that interested me at all was the strange and never publicly explained kidnapping of the son of Frank Sinatra. And beyond newspaper accounts of kidnapping, there are all those accounts in literature, and for me as a youngster, certainly the most important of all those was Robert Louis Stevenson's. However, when I was still seventeen, on March 1, 1932, the son of Charles Augustus Lindbergh was abducted from the Lindbergh home in Hopewell, New Jersey. Less than five years before that day, Lindbergh had flown across the ocean alone in that airplane which now hangs suspended in the Smithsonian Institution. He crossed the ocean from west to east, as we all know, on May 21, 1927 and after his return to the United States, he went about the country. I saw Charles Augustus Lindbergh riding in an open car and I ran after it trying to get closer to this living image of courage and romance. Charles Lindbergh and his trip across the ocean was, and is, something very real to me. After all, he crossed the ocean when I was just thirteen years old.

I can remember that after his return from Europe he made a ceremonial flight for the United States Mail Service. He'd been one of the early air-mail pilots before he soloed to Paris and so this later flight was in the character of a sentimental journey. I was a freshman in high school at the time and my history teacher, Mr. Alvin E. Rutenbeck, encouraged us to invest the twenty-five cents for the special air-mail stamp, and address a postcard, via St. Louis, to ourselves. We addressed our postcards in Mr. Rutenbeck's American History class one afternoon while he wrote on the board a suggested message that we could send to ourselves. The message read: Lindy says use air-mail; let's do it, be modern. We all mailed our cards and I must admit that I waited rather impatiently for mine to return to me, which it did; and as I sit here thinking about this, I wish I had that card now, but I don't. I gave it to my brother's son when he was thirteen years old and that's some time ago, too.

So, Charles Augustus Lindbergh was a very real person to me back in 1932 and, in my own way, I admired him extremely. This was, of course, years before Lindbergh made that trip to Germany and came back to report to all Americans that the German military machine was of such size and might that the only role for America was one of appeasement. But in 1932 Lindbergh still was to me pretty much what he had been back on May 21, 1927; and 1932 was the year his infant son was kidnapped. I remember following the story in the press all through the offering of the fifty thousand dollars in ransom money, through the finding of some of the ransom money on Bruno Richard Hauptmann, through the long, drawn-out trial, through the finding of the battered body of the baby more than two years after the kidnapping and, finally, Hauptmann's execution, more than two years after that.

Until the body of the Lindbergh baby was found, I had a strong willful hope that it would turn up in the care of some mysterious person. Like I'm sure was true of all kinds of other people, I hoped that the whole occurrence was not actually real—that it was some kind of ceremonial act, primitive and awful but still without actual and final truth. I would like to be able to say here that what I had hoped for, way back then, was that this kidnapping was only symbolic in some way—that, really, it didn't take place, that the whole event was a kind of art form or witchcraft, and that the art form would be seen for what it was—a work of art, a frightful play, and not reality and that the witchcraft, if that's what it was, would be undone either by breaking the spell or by a simple application of reason. I wish I could truthfully say that back then I had wished that the kidnapping of the Lindbergh baby was only as symbolic as the traditional act we describe as "burning in effigy," but I don't know that I had so specific a wish. However, I do know that on that evening in that room in Florence, when the words "kidnapped a child in effigy," appeared on the paper before me, I was thinking of the Lindbergh kidnapping of thirty-two years before.

In stanza five of the poem, I make point of the official penchant for quantitative exactness and how this works against the possibility of responding to anything not pre-programmed—like hearing the loudly trumpeted word, "Jelly."

At five, by a timepiece ignited by a dead President
From the bowl of fire at the Olympics,
They queued up to a shake or trill and galloped behind
An overlapping spur,
While his last trumpeted jelly came hallooing back from the hills
    around,
Unsullied and unheard.

The first two lines of this stanza owe at least part of their existence to an event that took place in May of 1933. That was the month in which the "Century of Progress," or the World's Fair of 1933, opened in Chicago. That was the year, also, that I was particularly reminded of the astronomy lectures Mr. August F. W. Kringle used to give all of us kids at the Milwaukee County Home for Dependent Children every Thursday night, back in 1930 and 1931—if it didn't rain. Mr. Kringle, called Chris Kringle at Christmastime, was the seventy-year-old superintendent of the home when I was there. He'd been born in Virginia and taught rural school in the South before he got the job of running what amounted to a kind of orphanage out there on the outskirts of Wauwatosa, Wisconsin. With all of his good qualities, and he had several, he was still a narrow, lascivious old man with a broad streak of the sadistic in him.

I was fifteen when the county welfare people caught up with us five kids who were living alone after Mother died and no one, not even the law, knew where Pa was. We were all taken to the Detention Home for a few days and then on out to the Home for Dependent Children. That was in October of 1930, and on the first Thursday night that I was there Mr. Kringle had all the boys and girls—there were about three hundred of us—stand around him on the grass outside the building that looked like a nineteenth-century Massachusetts shoe factory but was called the "Boys' Cottage." After it became as silent as three hundred tombs, Mr. Kringle pointed up to the sky and said that that was Betelgeuse up there. He said that that bright star was part of the constellation of Orion, that it was about two hundred and forty light years from the earth, and that it was one of the fine evidences of God's handiwork. Then he pointed out the dipper and asked us to follow in a line from the last two stars in the handle. There, he said, was the star, Arcturus. He said it was an old star and that it was discussed in the Bible, in the Book of Job. Among the stars whose names, I suppose, I'll never forget are Betelgeuse and Arcturus.

Mr. Kringle pointed out a lot of other stars that first night, but I really didn't see but a few of them because for much of the time I was watching the lights of cars passing on the Watertown Plank Road below. That was the real world, down there, and as far as I was concerned I was as far from that world as I was from Betelgeuse or Arcturus. After quoting something from Sir James Jeans and a long passage from the Bible which proved that Sir James Jeans was correct, we filed back into the boys' cottage and sat down in the playroom, boys on one side and girls on the other of the wide middle aisle. Mr. Kringle took his place at the front of the room and began asking questions. After each question, he'd point at someone in the room and they were expected to answer.

When he asked the question if man would ever make anything as beautiful as a star, he pointed at me. As was the custom, I stood up. I must not have answered fast enough because Mr. Kringle said, "Come on now, boy, come on."

I finally answered, "I don't know."

Mr. Kringle asked me to repeat what I'd said and I did. I again stated, "I don't know."

"You're a new boy, aren't you?" he asked and I answered, "Yes, sir," as if he were a policeman.

"What's your name?" he inquired and I told him my name was Donald Weismann.

"That's a German name, isn't it?" he asked.

I said that my father's father had come from Germany and my mother was Scotch-Irish.

"Now I want to ask you again, boy," Mr. Kringle said, beginning to get red in the face. "Will any human being ever make such a beautiful thing as Betelgeuse or Arcturus?"

"I don't know," I answered.

Then Mr. Kringle walked to the center aisle and halfway down to where I was standing and said, "Well believe me, boy, your father might have been German and your mother might have been—what did you say she was?" And I said she was Scotch-Irish. "And your mother may have been Scotch-Irish, but you, boy, you're a smart aleck. Now you come on over, you get yourself in my office at eight o'clock in the morning and I want to do some talking to you."

I don't know or I can't remember what happened between that time and when we were dismissed and went on up to the dormitory to bed, but it was made clear to me, while we were standing in line to brush our teeth and while we were neatly folding our orange corduroy pants and gray flannel shirts over the foot of the bed, that there was no picnic ahead for me in Superintendent Kringle's office the following morning.

After breakfast and after mowing a patch of the expansive front lawn, I walked over to Mr. Kringle's office. A portly woman directed me to sit down on an orange-colored varnished bench. After about fifteen minutes, Mr. Kringle came in and acted as if I wasn't even there. He went about his work, answered the telephone, made some telephone calls, did some writing, farted a lot, talked to some other people in the office, left the office and returned—all without acknowledging my presence in any way.

At about ten o'clock he looked up from some papers on his desk and said, "Come over here, boy."

I said, "Yes, sir," and walked up to the front of his desk.

"No," he instructed, "around here," motioning that I should come to a position at his left behind the desk. Then suddenly he jerked open the top drawer, reached in and pulled out a very small grain. He held it between his trembling fingers and shoved it toward my eyes. "What is this?" he demanded.

"I think it's a grain of wheat," I guessed, "or maybe it's an oat."

"It's wheat," he confirmed; and then still holding it in front of my eyes, he asked, "Can you make anything like this?"

And I said, "No sir."

"Can anyone make something like this?"

"No."

"Will anyone ever be able to make something like this?" he continued.

And I said that I didn't know.

Mr. Kringle became almost apoplectic; he began to shout and beat his fists on the desk.

"Now you get that chair over there, boy, and you bring it up here, right here," he said, pointing to a place right alongside of him. I got the chair and he said, "Now sit down there, boy." So I sat down. Then Mr. Kringle leaned toward me, put his face a few inches from mine and then with both hands raised the upper and lower lids of his left eye. "Now I want you to look in there, boy," he said. "Now you go ahead and look in that eye, go ahead and look."

And so I looked into Mr. Kringle's eye. It was like an oyster with thin threads of red and purple running around in it. It seemed to get bigger as I looked and the pupil seemed to pulsate. I began to feel wet and cold.

"Now tell me straight, boy," Mr. Kringle said, his ancient breath against my face. "Can anyone make an eye like that?"

"No, sir."

"Will anyone ever be able to make an eye like that?"

"No, sir."

"Now that's better, boy," Mr. Kringle said. "Now you go sit on that bench until the lunch bell rings."

And after a long time it did. The dessert was a tapioca pudding and it looked like hundreds of Mr. Kringle's left eye looking up at me, and over the side of the bowl, like snails, at everyone.

So, Mr. August F. W. Kringle showed me a grain of wheat, his left eye, Betelgeuse and Arcturus and these have been with me in very special ways ever since.

When the Century of Progress opened in Chicago three years later, it was opened in a unique way. The President of the United States, Franklin D. Roosevelt, pushed a button and by means of a photo-electric cell, a beam from the star Arcturus, which had been received in a telescope at Yerkes Observatory at Williams Bay, Wisconsin, was made to turn on the lights and signal the opening of that World's Fair. At the time, I thought it was a pretty neat trick and a fine thing for FDR to be doing. At the time, too, I was reminded of Mr. Kringle standing out there on the lawn in front of the boys' cottage and pointing his finger up at the star that was destined to light up a Century of Progress.

Now, on either side of 1933, the year the Fair opened, there were the Olympic games of 1932, held in Los Angeles and the Olympic games of 1936, held in Berlin. Both of these were commenced by igniting a bowl of slow-burning material from a torch carried to the games by the Olympic messenger. So, after all I've said here, it should seem rather more ordinary than curious that in stanza five of my poem, I wrote "At five, by a timepiece ignited by a dead President / From the bowl of fire at the Olympics."

Stanza six of the poem gets our yelling protagonist to Cleveland, Ohio:

Yelling jelly into the wind, for who knows where
A dark-adapted protectively colored wayfaring intimate
May bend his ear,
He rode the rods below the oldest reefer of the Nickel Plate
To night in Cleveland's yard.

The term, dark-adapted, which appears in the second line of this stanza fell easily to hand, mainly because of two sets of experiences which are still alive in me. The first was afforded me when I was in officer's training school with the United States Navy at Harvard University in 1942.

After a period of several months as a Civilian Specialist Instructor with the Army Air Forces Technical Training Command, I was commissioned an Ensign in the United States Naval Reserve by long distance telephone. As per instructions, I secured a copy of the official *Navy Regulations,* purchased United States Naval officers uniforms, including raincoat and greatcoat, practiced saluting in front of a mirror, and got on a train for Boston. At Harvard University I underwent a course aimed at preparing me to be a United States Naval Communications Officer. I did so well in the course that I was one of a few to be given an extra month of training for special work aboard aircraft carriers. The fact that I was finally shipped out of the country as a Communications Officer with an amphibious outfit and did duty with what was called a JASCO (which then stood for, and perhaps still stands for, Joint Assault Signal Company), and lived in foxholes and landing craft, doesn't matter now and really has no place here. What does have a place is that during the training period at Harvard University we were expected to learn to identify a great variety of American and foreign ships under very poor light conditions. To facilitate this, the navy had constructed in a former classroom, a stage set that resembled open sky and water. Along the horizon of this tableau, it was possible to cause very exactly constructed models of Japanese ships and German, Italian, Russian, Canadian and American ships to move slowly along. As Communications Officers, we were told we would be responsible for identifying ships even before they hove over the horizon and into full view. We were told that quick identification was often the difference between having the other ship sink us, or our sinking the other ship—or in the case of both ships being friendly, no one sinking anybody.

Before entering the room in which this tableau was displayed, we were required to sit in an adjoining room in pitch darkness. And after sitting there for a good length of time, we stumbled our ways into the room with the artificial sea and the artificial sky and the beautiful model ships. This room, like the immediately adjoining ready-room, was in pitch darkness. Then a voice from somewhere in the black announced that very shortly a red dot would appear directly ahead and that all of us should look at that small red dot. So far as I know, no one living or dead could be sure that all, few, or any of the fresh ensigns in that room really looked at the red dot. As I remember, I strained hard and saw it right away. I took it all quite seriously, for after all, a quick and correct identification of some still-to-be-seen ship could mean that I got back home or not. The purpose of the red dot was to focus the fledgling officers' eyes on the center of the tableau. Then after a little while, lights—perhaps controlled by a rheostat—began to light the scene, first very weakly and then gradually building up until the tableau was in something like half-light. Our success or failure in this exercise was measured by whether or not we could properly identify the ship on the horizon before the light was raised to a certain intensity. I got pretty good at this, and in fact, I enjoyed it.

It was like being out on the ocean without having to be out on the ocean. Later on in the Bismarck and the China Seas, it was like being on the ocean when I most certainly was on the ocean.

But that's not the point I want to make here. The point I want to make is that before we were herded into the room in which the tableau was set up, we had been what is called "dark-adapted." We all know what that means: simply that the longer you stay in the dark, the more you can see in the dark. What surprised me, however, was how very, very much more one can see in the dark if he remains in it for a long time and then tips his head back to bring whatever light there might be to those rods of the retina which are ordinarily less taxed and hence fresher and more receptive than the rods which receive light when the head and eyes are in more normal positions. It seemed I had known this all informally long before being in the navy. I remembered when I was in the hospital at the Home for Dependent Children a dozen years before, and used to go up to the third floor where my favorite night nurse, Frances Shudolc, a young Slovenian from Eveleth, Minnesota, would take her break between midnight and about a quarter to one. We used to sit close on a wide windowsill and talk and look out to the north over the rolling countryside. And with no lights burning on that floor and with nothing but starlight outside, after a while I could see rabbits running all over.

After the war I went to the Ohio State University at Columbus on the G.I. Bill of Rights to get my Ph.D. In the School of Art there was a man named Hoyt S. Sherman who had discovered a new procedure for teaching drawing. He had constructed a huge room, one end of which was occupied by an immense screen. At the other end of the room there was a battery of high-powered projectors which were used to throw huge images on the screen. Above the projectors he had a platform which ran from one side of the room to the other, and which resembled the conning bridge of a ship. It was on this bridge that Professor Sherman held station during classroom instruction.

Now the way this drawing class worked was something like this: the students enrolled in the class went first to a dark room where they remained until they were properly dark-adapted. Then, just as in the navy situation, they stumbled into the large, dark projection room. Each student found a position at a piece of furniture that, if you could see it, resembled a lectern with a very large, slanted top. On each of these lecterns there was a pad of newsprint on which the students would be expected to draw. Recorded music played continuously during the drawing lesson. With the students in the room and at their respective positions, and having been properly dark-adapted, Professor Sherman, using controls said to have been specially carved to fit his hands by a dental student who switched to sculpture under Professor Sherman's influence—would flash an image on the screen for a very short period of time, something like a tenth of a second. This extraordinary blast of light on the retinas of eyes that had been in the dark for so long was nothing short of traumatic. After the blast of light the room fell pitch-dark again, and in that darkness the students were asked—were required—to try to reproduce the image they had seen on the screen. This procedure was repeated over and over during the class time of about thirty minutes. At the end of the period, and still in the darkness of what Professor Sherman called his "flash room," the students crumpled up their drawings and walked out of the classroom depositing the drawings in a large waste bin.

The pedagogical concept behind this, according to conversations I had with Professor Sherman, had to do with encouraging freedom of action and freedom of expression—both in the dark—without risk of criticism, disappointment or failure. In all fairness I must say that this course, which extended over six or eight weeks (I forget which), culminated in a procedure which allowed the student to see not only what he had done but also what the others had done. Also, in fairness I must say that Professor Sherman was concerned with something he called "seeing with perceptual unity"—not a bad thing at all. But his theories about this were voiced and written in a manner that could compare visually to an extremely valuable moth-eaten afghan. And through the afghan even I could recognize threads of gestalt psychology, the experiments in perception staged by Professor Ames at Princeton, and the practical applications of certain principles of gestalt psychology by Professor Renshaw who, incidentally, worked with the military during the Second World War in perfecting a system for rapid identification of aircraft.

So, I suppose that when I was writing my poem and got to a point where something was asked to be said about highly attuned individuals— individuals who might just hear the man as he yelled "jelly"—I fell upon the analogous situation of adaptation to the dark and used the hyphen- ated description, dark-adapted.

And, then, in the last two lines of stanza six, we have the man with the word riding the "rods below the oldest reefer of the Nickel Plate" into nighttime Cleveland, Ohio.

During the early years of the Great Depression, I used to spend time drawing and painting in places like Jones Island, just offshore from the south end of Milwaukee. At that time there were still the last shack remains of a fishing village on the island, and a canal at the east end where idled coal and iron ore boats were tied up and rusting. It was a wonderful place, forgotten, it seemed to everyone but the few remaining old fishermen and some ancient hobos who had taken up residence in the deserted shacks and rotting wooden hulks beached at the north end. There was a small saloon on the island and when my painting didn't go so well or when I had finished, I'd walk around to the saloon for a cold beer. And standing at the uneven bar in the cool dark shade of the place, I used to talk to the few fishermen and hobos who were always there. I'd never had much experience with, or love for, water—I hardly ever swam in Lake Michigan, and at that time I had yet to see any ocean—so I usu- ally ended up talking with the ex-knights of the road rather than with the ex-toilers of the sea.

In those days I wanted terribly to wander all over America to see the places I'd read and heard about and all the others, too. I wanted to walk around in Wyoming and see the San Fernando Valley, the gold mines of Nova Scotia, and I wanted to know Albuquerque, the place my father had said years before was the greatest place on the face of the earth. He used to say that the longest trains ever made up passed through Albuquerque and that the sun was always shining there. People didn't ask you your name in Albuquerque, he said, and there was plenty of space in which to lose or find yourself.

So, standing there at the bar of the saloon on Jones Island, I listened to those old, old hobos who, like my father, had ridden freight trains up and down and back and forth across America. Their descriptions of the places and towns they'd been in always made long horizontal pictures in my mind. Everything they talked about had a way of seeming to string along on either side of railroad tracks. And they talked a lot about box-cars, open and shut, about tank cars, flat cars, and gondolas all high-balling along. They talked about riding the tops of boxcars, far back from the engine out of the smoke and flying cinders, up in the good, free air. They talked about railroad bulls, with billy clubs as long as axe handles, and how you learned to stay out of their sight.

The safest place to ride, I remember their telling me, was underneath the cars—across the widely spaced open steel trusses that used to support every kind of railroad car until they started building them on a floor of solid steel girders. All you do, one hobo told me, is carry a few slats with you, lay them across the trusses, roll out your bundle, and once the train is out of the yard, you can just go off to sleep, safe between the floor of the car and the roadbed about a foot and a half below you. This is what they called "riding the rods"—riding the trusses below the old wooden cars. In my poem, I have the man with the word riding those rods, and I have him riding underneath a reefer, which is no more than a name for a refrigerator car. I make this car the property of a particular railroad line, the Nickel Plate, whose tracks still run into Cleveland, Ohio. But all this didn't come only from listening to my father, or by talking with hobos on Jones Island. It took the experience of a long trip, begun on foot, to force me to ride my first freight train—out of Hoboken, New Jersey, as it hap-pened. And since much of the narrative quality of my poem depends on simple physical movement through the American landscape, I tell of this particular trip in some detail.

The opening for that unforeseen trip came in June of 1933 when I was invited to go with my former high school art teacher, Alexander Tillotson, and his wife to spend the summer painting in St. Ignace,

Michigan. We drove up north from Milwaukee in Mr. Tillotson's black 1931 two-door Chevrolet sedan. In St. Ignace they rented a house and after a couple of days things were running pretty much on schedule. We got up early in the morning, Mrs. Tillotson cooked a big breakfast, and then Mr. Tillotson and I took off in the car to find subjects for our paintings of that day. This worked very well for about a week and then something got hold of me. I didn't want to stay in St. Ignace and I didn't want to paint. Maybe it had something to do with the fact that I admired Mr. Tillotson's painting so much, and as I watched him those first few days go about his work so methodically and with such fine success, my own efforts felt stupid and worthless to me.

So, toward the end of the week we had breakfast as usual and Mr. Tillotson and I piled into his car with our painting materials. He parked the car on the north edge of town, took out his easel, paints, and canvas and walked to the place from which, on the day before, he'd begun a large painting. I didn't take my painting materials from the car. I told Mr. Tillotson that I was going to walk around a while and just look. Empty-handed, I walked out beyond the town, out about a mile on the gravel road that runs to the north and stood there for a while. It must have been about nine in the morning. The sun was low and the sky was clear. I stood there feeling wonderfully and absolutely alone. I was eighteen. I could hear birds singing and the rush of the wind across my ears. Then a car came along and stopped right beside me. The driver leaned across the front seat and asked "Where you going? I'm going as far as the Soo." And then, perhaps because I didn't answer right away, the driver added, "To the Soo—Sault Saint Marie," I knew that one Sault Saint Marie was in Ontario and that was across the line in Canada, and as I stood there looking at the stranger in the car, I felt that of all the places I must go, I must go to Sault Saint Marie and go now. And as easy as anything in the world, I opened the car door and got in.

As we drove along with all the windows open and the wind whipping around me, I felt a tremendous freedom shot through with real terror. Already I had thoughts of Mr. Tillotson looking for me in an hour or so and wondering how I was doing. This worried me and I resolved that as soon as I got to the Sault and looked around just a little bit, I'd turn and get back to St. Ignace. But it didn't work out that way. The driver let me out on the main street of Sault Saint Marie, Ontario and I walked right out of town to the gravel road that runs east and west across Canada. I stood there looking down that road to the east where the sun was still pushing up and I thought of the Atlantic Ocean. Across the road, seven shunted boxcars stood wide open and empty. The name CANADIAN PACIF-IC showed out bright white against the dark red color of the wooden cars. I looked down the road to the west and thought of the Pacific lying out there. I kept standing there in my summer shoes, my light-colored cotton khaki trousers and cotton shirt, and felt around in my pockets. I had ten dollars and ten cents—all my money for that entire summer—and a green and white Milwaukee streetcar ticket. I took it out and read the familiar overprinted red letters, TMER&L CO., which stood for The Milwaukee Electric Railway and Light Company, and remembered how when we were very little we used to sing out other words to those letters as the streetcars went by back home: Tim Murphey Eats Rats and Likes Cooked Onions. I put the ticket back in my pocket, put my great and everlasting friend, Alexander Tillotson, out of my mind and started walking east.

Then, like the beginning of some old movie, a car appeared out of the west and kept coming closer, trailing a long plume of dust. It slowed down, it stopped, and I got in. The driver said he was going to Echo Bay and I said that that's where I was going. On the other side of Echo Bay, another car picked me up and took me to Thessalon. That night I slept in an old boat pulled up on the shore just outside of a place called Blind River, and nearly froze to death. The next day in Sudbury, Ontario, I bought a woolen shirt for five dollars and a blue denim jacket for ninety-eight cents. On most of the remaining four dollars plus, I went through Sturgeon Falls, North Bay, Mattawa, Pembroke, Ottawa, and to some place about fifty miles west of Montreal.

I forget the name of the place, but I know that the last of the day was running out when I got there. Then, like in that same old movie, the black silhouette of another car loomed out of the afterglow. It was going at a good clip and it shot right by, but I noticed that the driver had taken a hard look at me. About half a mile down the road the car turned around and then passed me again, very slowly, only to make another U-turn, come back, and stop right where I was standing. The car was a 1930 Bentley roadster with a right-hand drive and a spiral brass horn mounted on the outside.

"Are you wishing a ride?" the driver asked.

"Yes sir," I said.

"How far are you going?"

"To Montreal."

"Don't you have any baggage?"

"I have it here in my pockets."

"Come around and get in," the driver said. "I'm not going all the way to Montreal; I'm going to Hudson Heights but that's only a few miles this side of the city."

Even before he had the car in second gear, he asked me what my name was and I told him.

"Uh-huh," he said, and then for at least ten miles he didn't say a word. I kept looking straight through the windshield, but out the corner of my eye I could see his hands on the steering wheel. They were in what appeared to me to be very beautiful dark brown leather gloves. He was wearing a light tan tweed suit and knitted socks with a diamond pattern. His shoes were thick-soled, soft-appearing leather, dark brown and matte polished. The car purred along magnificently and the sky ahead ran its course of deepening blue-violets.

And then after what seemed to be a very long time, the driver said, "My name is E. P. Gausden, and I suppose you wonder why I stopped for you."

"No," I replied. "I don't wonder, I just thought that you wanted to help someone out."

"Yes. That may be partly it, but it's much more than that." And then without giving me time to make any response, Mr. Gausden explained, "You know that place you were standing—where I picked you up, I mean? Well, young man, just a month ago my son was killed . . . on a

bicycle there—and, you . . . Donald . . . you look exactly like my son—
I thought you were my son standing there."

I don't know that I said anything after Mr. Gausden told me that,
and then he asked how old I was.

"I'm eighteen," I answered.

"The same age," Mr. Gausden noted. "Where are you going in
Montreal?"

"To my brother's house on St. Jacques Street. He's sick," I lied.

"Will you stay in Montreal?"

"Only for a little while. I'm going to Nova Scotia."

"What will you do there?" he wondered.

"I'm going to work in the gold mines."

"Where is your home, Donald?"

"I was born in Milwaukee, Wisconsin," I said.

"Your speech tells me you've gone on to school."

"Yes, I was in my last year of college when I left home."

Mr. Gausden asked, "Mustn't you go back to finish?"

"Oh, I don't know."

"Do you like sports?"

"I like to run," I said.

"What distances do you run?"

"Oh, I never ran in any meets or anything like that," I explained. "I
just like to run."

"That's fine," Mr. Gausden said, "just fine."

In memory, right now, I can still see Mr. Gausden driving the car in
the light from the dash, looking a very healthy fifty years old, handsome,
secure, but still suffering what I would now count one of the greatest loss-
es imaginable. And even though I knew then what a delicate thing it was
to be sitting next to Mr. Gausden in that Bentley roadster, where I could
presume his son had sat not many weeks before, still I felt imprecarious-
ly at ease, and Mr. Gausden and I talked freely and even laughed a lot.

Then for some reason Mr. Gausden appeared to get uneasy. Our conversation became a little stilted and then both of us fell silent. After a
while Mr. Gausden said, "I want to take you to Hudson Heights with me

tonight. I want you to meet Mrs. Gausden. Will you come and stay the night with us? After all, it's late and I can drive you to St. Jacques Street when I go to work in the morning. Won't you stay the night with us?"

In those days I was not ready to stay overnight in almost anyone's house but my own. I hadn't as yet become at ease with all the things that one does with grace in someone else's house. Into my mind came very uncomfortable pictures centering about the use of the bathroom, getting up in the morning, and eating breakfast with Mr. and Mrs. Gausden, all the while I was hoping to be back on the road going east.

"Yes," I said, "it would be nice to stay overnight in your house."

"That's perfect," Mr. Gausden said.

In Hudson Heights, he took a left turn off the wide road and we started up a narrower winding one with well-kept grounds on either side. "This is it," Mr. Gausden said. "We'll be at the house in less than five minutes." And in a few minutes he became more animated and blew three times on the brass horn. Then we were up on top of what I still remember as a small mesa. There were lights around a rambling, one-story house, the outside covered with very wide clapboards stained almost black. A woman came out in a long white dress, flanked by two large white dogs. Mr. Gausden stopped in front of her and from out of nowhere a man appeared who stood waiting as Mr. Gausden got out of the car.

"I've brought someone with me," Mr. Gausden said to the woman in white. "His name is Donald Weismann. He's from Milwaukee and he's on his way to see his brother in the city."

I got out of the car and stood with the car between Mrs. Gausden and me. The man who had suddenly appeared slipped into the driver's seat and drove the car away. Then for a long moment the three of us just stood there.

Mrs. Gausden looked at me and then at Mr. Gausden. "His name is Donald?" she asked. "Donald what?"

"Donald Weismann," Mr. Gausden answered, "and he's going to stay the night with us."

Mrs. Gausden looked at me and proved that everything Mr. Gausden had said about their son was true. And so there you stand again, part of something you might never know, and so all you do is wait.

"Oh, come in," she welcomed, and then she turned to Mr. Gausden. "Oh, I'm so glad, Eric."

Mrs. Gausden quickly excused herself and just as quickly disappeared into the house.

"You must be hungry," Mr. Gausden said to me. "It would be good if we ate something. We don't have to get up early in the morning, do we?"

We walked into what I gathered was the living room of the house. It was a large room with carved furniture, tables and chairs and cabinets in dark wood. On the walls I could see what appeared to be primitive wood carvings and a number of boomerangs. I must have looked rather hard at the room because Mr. Gausden explained, "I lived in Australia for a while and I brought these things back. There was a time when I could throw those boomerangs."

Then, just as suddenly as she had disappeared, Mrs. Gausden reappeared and said, "You'll want a bath before we have some tea, come."

She showed me to the bathroom and I went in and closed the door. The floor creaked a little, so I just stood quietly for a while taking in this bathroom that was bigger than any bedroom in any of the houses I'd lived with my family. And all the while the Canadian landscape stretched out across the back of my mind, endless, dark, with one long gravel road and the train tracks glistening alongside.

The bath had been half drawn and there was a pair of pajamas and a robe laid out for me. I undressed, finished filling the bathtub with deliciously warm water and stepped into the tub. On a shelf within reach there was an array of bath salts. One of them smelled like spice and lilac but with something strong behind it like leather or oak and I dumped an awful lot of it into the water. In the fragrance, in the perfect temperature of the room, in my fatigue, curiosity and exhilaration, I had one of the greatest baths of my life. And then I dried and tried on the pajamas, which fit perfectly, and the robe, which fit exactly so. Now, I had to go out of this sanctuary. When I opened the door Mr. Gausden was a few feet down the hall.

"Oh, good, Donald," he said. "Come."

Mrs. Gausden was sitting at a small table on which there was a silver teapot and some cakes in a silver dish. She stood up and took my hand as I came in and then asked me to sit across from her. Over the tea we talked for an hour or so about Montreal, about Hudson Heights, about where I'd come from and where I was going, whether my brother was very sick or just sick so-so, and why in the world I should be wanting to go to the gold mines of Nova Scotia. Mr. Gausden talked about Australia and he talked about Germany and the United States, and I learned that he was the head of a publishing firm in Montreal and that his work required that he go to Europe at least twice a year. We talked long enough for me to say that I could draw and paint and that I had always wanted to be an artist.

But the longer we sat over tea, the more it became clear to me that my importance was that of a ghost in the house. I wondered about their dead son, what he had done and how he really looked, but there was no way for me to ask. Instead I let my mind wander off to thoughts of those boomerangs on the wall, who had made them, when and where; and how one throws them, who had thrown them, and if they'd ever be thrown again. I must have looked tired, and after a while Mrs. Gausden suggested that I had perhaps had a busy day and that I might like to go to bed. When I smiled, she got up, took me by the arm, led me to the bedroom, and said good night. I slept the sleep of the virtuous that night, and I slept that counterfeit sleep on a bed softer than any bed I'd ever lain in, with my head on pillows more pleasantly cool and congenial than any I had ever known.

The morning was full of sunshine in a room back from a terrace that overlooked a great part of the countryside. The breakfast was served by a young woman who spoke with an Irish accent and among the things she set out were potatoes and meat. And when it was over and we were standing outside the house the man who had taken the car the night before drove it up and opened the door for me. Mrs. Gausden walked with me to the side of the car, took my hand, kissed me, and said something I couldn't hear. Mr. Gausden got in, started the car, turned, and drove down the driveway away from Hudson Heights.

Nothing much was said all the way into downtown Montreal and then Mr. Gausden said, "What number on St. Jacques Street?"

I said I'd forgotten exactly, but "Up there," pointing through the windshield. "Up there; if you'll just leave me off there, I know how to get to the house."

He stopped the car in front of a small bakery shop, and asked, "Do you mean here?"

I said, "Yes, this is just fine," and I moved to get out of the car.

Mr. Gausden put his hand on my arm and said, "Good God, Donald, you can't leave Montreal, you must stay. I have a big publishing plant, and we have artists who work for us. You could work for us, you could stay in Montreal, you could work here, live with us. You're not sure at all, are you, that you want to go back to Milwaukee anyway, and the gold mines of Nova Scotia really don't operate anymore, Donald."

And there you are again, across some inches from another human being whose plight you sympathize with entirely, but about which, you can do nothing without changing your whole life.

"It's true, Mr. Gausden." I said, "I must go, I'm late already; I told my brother I'd be here two days ago."

"You'll come back, won't you?"

"When I come back from Nova Scotia."

"How long will you stay with your brother?"

"I don't know. Maybe a day, or two, or three."

"Well," Mr. Gausden said, handing me a small card. "You'll call me before you leave; will you?"

"Yes," I said and then I got out of the car.

It was raining a little now and the street was full of reflections. Mr. Gausden drove off and I read his telephone number on the engraved card. It was the same, 7193, as my father's when he owned the Adept Window Cleaning Company back in Milwaukee.

That afternoon I crossed Vermont and New Hampshire and into

Maine on my way to the gold mines of Nova Scotia. I never called Mr. Gausden and I never came through Montreal on my way back. When I returned I crossed into the United States at Rouses Point, New York and went on down to New York City, to the New York of 1933.

My last hitched ride ended at 192nd Street and I walked into Times Square where I bought a glass of orange juice and an ice cream cone. After that I still had about forty cents in my pocket and the Milwaukee streetcar ticket. I recall leaning against the little wooden ice cream stand and trying to make the five-cent cone last as long as possible. I thought of how now I'd be able to tell that I'd been to New York, to Times Square, when I got back; but I was beginning to worry how I'd ever make it over the thirteen or fourteen hundred miles of highway to the edge of Milwaukee, where I could use the streetcar ticket to get me back to the Tillotson's house where I'd been staying since leaving the Home for Dependent Children. And there was no one at the other end to pull me in. I hurried to the river and crossed to Hoboken. And there everything changed for the worse—just miles and miles of city pavement, strewn with paper blowing in the dust; no way to hitchhike, no one even noticing that I was there. Night came and I was still in Hoboken. So far as I could tell, there was just one way for me to get back to Milwaukee on that forty cents and that was by hopping a freight train.

The freight yards spread out under floodlights mounted on tall poles. I remembered that the phrase "hopping a freight" means exactly that: you shouldn't climb into a boxcar that's not moving and wait for the engine to pull you on out; you should find the train you want and wait until it starts to roll, and then when there's no longer time for the railroad bulls to get you, you run alongside and hop onto the car. So I stood there in the Hoboken yard with no way of telling which string of cars would begin to move or to where it might go. I stood in the shadow of a locomotive that must have been used during the day and its boiler was cooling down. The engine gave off high-pitched pings and low-pitched clunks as I waited in the dark. Then, one of the strings of cars began to move, and as I watched I became so scared that all I did was huddle deeper in the shadow and closer to the warmth of the cooling engine. The string rolled slowly past and I could see the rods underneath. I wondered how in God's name anyone could get in under the car and onto those rods while the train was moving. Nothing that I could remember and nothing that I could imagine gave me any reason to believe that that operation was humanly possible. So for the next few hours I watched short and long lines of cars move one way or another away from me. Then, suddenly, as if possessed, I shot out of the shadow and ran full tilt alongside one of them. I hadn't known until then how difficult it is to keep upright in the loose gravel—and with all that wind and noise. Snatches of stories filled with images of men and boys stumbling and rolling under the wheels of the cars, legless, armless, pieces not enough to fill a peach basket, flashed through my mind. Still I ran searching for an open car that I could throw myself up and into. There weren't any, so I grabbed the ladder of one of the last closed cars and climbed halfway up, so as not to be silhouetted against the last of the yard lights. The train picked up speed much faster than I ever thought something of that length and weight could, and before long the train was highballing along.

With the lights of the yard far behind, I climbed onto the top of the car. There was a moon out and I could see the locomotive far up ahead, and for the first time I felt hot cinders coming against me. For a while I just sat panting on those three boards of the catwalk. The sky was almost cloudless and a fifty to sixty mile wind was blowing at me. For a while I felt safe, even good, and then I knew I was very cold. The train was pushing into the Appalachians by now, and looking down I could see brilliantly flashing moon reflections in rivers and little lakes and ponds. I had the feeling of traveling through El Greco's *Toledo*, and I kept getting colder and colder and then very drowsy. I pulled my socks up over the bottoms of my trouser legs, lay down with my head facing the caboose, wedged my arms under the catwalk to keep from rolling off and tried to fight off sleep.

I woke up in Hornell, New York where they coupled on some more cars, including some tankers. Once we got rolling again, I worked my way to one of the tankers, got down to it and for a moment enjoyed the windbreak made by the high reefer just ahead. I stood on the low catwalk holding on to that pipe rail that runs around most tankers, and stretched my aching back. And then again I felt sleep coming down around, so I unbuckled my pants belt, passed the end around the pipe rail, and rebuckled it. Now, if I fell asleep and went down I'd remain suspended there.

And then I heard voices, loud threatening voices. I opened my eyes. The sun was shining, the train had stopped, and I was dangling from the railing by my pants belt. Two railroad bulls were standing on the reddish roadbed yelling at me, "How far you want to go, boy? Eternity? If that's where you want to go, boy, I can sure as hell send you there. Now, you get the hell off that car, and get your ass off the line or I'll take you on a road we got ready for punks like you," one of them said.

So while I unhitched my belt, he was telling me about it.

"It's a long straight roadbed, and it ain't for sleep," he said, "and ain't gravel, either. The ties are laid in busted bottles just for guys like you, and a couple of great beaters get back of you with baseball bats, and they say: boy, take off your shoes 'cause we're gonna chase you up that line, and we're gonna chase you till all your friends are gonna call you Stumpy 'cause your legs are gonna end where they come out of your guts." I got unhitched, grabbed up my pants and took off into the high weeds.

That night I got a freight out of Buffalo, a really fast one, and that was the one that took me to Cleveland, Ohio. From engine to caboose it was painted in the special letters of the Nickel Plate line and it brought me into Cleveland, Ohio just like I say in the poem, except that I didn't ride the rods; I rode the top of the "oldest reefer" into Cleveland.

———————————————

Stanza seven starts out with these three lines:

Where the tracks brake-shine under
The ferro-concrete arch named nineteen-oh-nine,
Big and square in a recessed panel,

I recall very clearly where the hyphenated words, brake-shine, came
from. Actually I had never heard these words until I was ready to leave
Cleveland. These words were given to me by a black man, and this is how
it happened.

I wanted to get out of Cleveland as fast as I could, so in the morning
I was back in that low valley in the heart of industrial Cleveland where
I'd come in the night before and which, in the poem, I allude to as
"Cleveland's yard." I wandered around in that wasteland, threaded with
tracks and scarred with abandoned buildings, trying to figure out where
the west-bound freights might stop or at least slow down enough to hop.
The sun was shining and it was warm, so I was surprised when I came
around one of the boxcars to find an old, bald-headed man sewing buttons on an overcoat.

He looked up. "You look like you're in a hurry," he said. "That's
always a dangerous way to be. Where's your home, son?"

"Milwaukee," I said.

"And you're in an awful hurry to get there, ain't you? Sit down here
and take it easy, son; winter's coming but there's still plenty of time."

And with that, the old man reached into one of his jacket pockets
and pulled out a round Copenhagen snuff can. He laid the can carefully

in the palm of his left hand and with his right deftly removed the cover. Inside the can was a large round pocket watch with its crystal missing. He looked at the watch, then at the sun, and then with his index finger he carefully moved the minute hand backwards so that the watch read ten minutes to nine instead of nine.

"Plenty of time," the old man said, putting the box back into his pocket. "I remember that I was once in an awful hurry out in Nevada. The guy came home while I was saying good-bye to her in the kitchen and I ran out the back door straight into a swarm of bees. I was stung all over and I itched and scratched and I nearly died. Never hurry," he said. "Never hurry, son, there's plenty of time."

"But I've really got to get home," I argued.

"'Tain't good to be anxious. What's the matter with just living here in Cleveland?"

"I don't know anybody in Cleveland," I said, "and this place isn't for me. All I want to find out is where the trains going west slow down enough to get on."

"I'd cool off if I was you," the old man replied, and he went back to sewing the button on his overcoat.

I walked down the line of cars and turned across a lot of tracks toward a little path that led up the side of a slag heap. I thought I heard someone singing and I stopped. It sounded like a lullaby, or blues, and it was coming from the top of the pile. I stood and listened for a while and the singing voice reminded me of years before when my father played very slow music on the mouth organ and his eyes fogged over as he said, "Now I'll play you a song about a man who lost his way and never found it again." And then my father, with a jelly glass cupped over the end of the mouth organ, played the saddest, slowest music I'd ever heard.

I followed it up the slag heap like one of the kids of Hamlin. There was a crazy white picket fence at the top and it ran around a shack built of tin signs and weathered boards. Out in the sun on a wooden box a huge black man sat facing away from me and singing to a tiny black girl. I think he must have heard me coming up the hill but he waited, and then, without losing his song, he turned and looked at me. I smiled; he smiled back and let the lullaby dwindle away.

"You comes from up or down?" he asked.

"I just came up. I was wondering where the trains going west slow down," I said.

"That's easy," the black man said. "You don't know yet how to tell where just any old train slows down? You see, it's a funny thing: the place where trains slows down is where they also speeds up, but that ain't no trouble at all, because you're interested to find yourself a slow train. Ain't that right?"

"Yes, that's right."

"Well, now," he said, "if a engine speeds up, that must mean it was just going slow before it started to speed up; ain't that right? And if a engine is slowing down, that must mean it was going fast, but ain't no more; ain't that right?"

"That's right," I agreed.

"Now it's a funny, natural thing," the black man continued, "that when a engine speeds up the wheels skid on the tracks. It's just the same when he puts on the brakes to slow down—the wheels skid on the tracks. Now, when an engine skids on the tracks, the wheels plain polishes them tracks; they makes them shine awful nice. It's my true experience for lots more years than you got, that where the trains goes slow is where the tracks shines. And now you say you wants to find yourself a train going west and that's slowed down, or just going slow. Right?"

"That's right."

"Well, I'm not going to worry you about freights pulled by engines that's getting up steam; I'm just going to let you know now where the westbound number is going slow. Yes, I'm going to tell you where them tracks brake-shines."

And with that, the big black man walked over to me and pointed down from his little mountain to a concrete bridge about a half-mile off. "You can almost see them shines from here," he said. "Now, you just go over there and wait on the other side of that bridge, and before it gets much later than now, you're going to hook yourself a ride out west. The engineer will be putting on the brakes over there, and them big wheels and them little wheels is going to be sliding and polishing them tracks just like you'll see it when you get there."

"Thank you," I said.

The black man squinted and looked off beyond anything to be seen. "And just as soon as this little one of mine," he said, waving to the little girl, "is big enough and smart enough to have herself a right man, then I'll be right back down there by that shine myself—been too long already."

"Yes," I said. "I sure do thank you; I better go now."

"You be careful," the big black man said. And as I went down the heap of slag to where the tracks brake-shine, I heard him singing again.

It was true, every bit of it; the tracks did brake-shine on the far side of that bridge. And the bridge was made of concrete, with iron reinforcements and so in the poem I call it a "ferro-concrete arch named nineteen-oh-nine" because there was a date enshrined there, as I remember, in a big sunken square panel, high on the arch where, were it a masonry bridge, the keystone would be.

It's true that I left Cleveland on a freight train and that I caught it under that ferro-concrete arch. In the poem, however, I have the man who shouts Jelly arrive at that place in Cleveland and depart in a "westbound cab." On arriving, however, "He eased from his knees to the gravel / And headed beneath the bridges for the square below the tower." I had him ease from his knees because he'd been riding the rods, and that's one way to get off of them. More important, however, was my concern to get him to that well-known square in Cleveland which in those days was marked by a building that culminated in a square tower high above the square. Something that wanted to be said about big city graft and the failing system of the Depression years comes out in the last three lines of the stanza in which the tower is said to have been "Built with a lot of hard arms and stolen bilk carried unclean / To the top in a hod with a perforated bottom / That failed to drain away the filth."

Stanzas eight, nine, ten and eleven derive from a variety of experiences but are brought together around my memory of that square and the one night I spent in Cleveland in 1933.

Night in the bilious grass of the square,
Criss-crossed with suicidewalks,
Sucked out bunches of hoarheads mixed
With the young defeated in their own success.
They stood around in slipknots wearing tin
Question marks arguing for no stakes between chewing.

In the stop-watched seconds when every body was silent,
Chewing or thumbnailing their far back teeth at once,
There was nothing but the weak din of the place
That could be sliced by voice easier than amber light the fog.
And in those seconds they stood between
Blank and tense, looking the same, but smelling different
To foxes and everything hunted.
Among them there was a brand of waiting
As if they'd been hurt in the gaps of their reason,
And to bridge the wound had found
A whipping-goat to flail with a swipple loaded with nails
And drive to trial for defecation of their undecipherable characters.

In this receptive blank, this
Waiting for waiting, no matter for what,
He who held the word could hope to have it heard,
So he told it through the din, then mushroomed it over the square
Like jelly inside the dome of the planetarium.

One wooden owl with mirror eyes planted
On a cornice of the courthouse
To scare away the chalk-loaded pigeons,
Tried to hoot as the word went out
Unheard, and its flock of echoes bleated away to din and died
As the silent chewing erupted again
In modulated belches and mouth muscle fussings that sounded
Something like but not language.

I'd arrived in Cleveland, as I said earlier, and was looking for a place
to stay. With all I'd heard about places for overnight transients being
maintained by the federal government in those years, I figured there must
be one not far, right there in Cleveland. I asked several men on the street
and got a variety of contradictory directions, so that around two in the
morning I was still looking when I came around a corner and ran smack
into a holdup. The man with the pistol appeared only mildly surprised
by my practically walking into him, and casually turned to me and said,
"Now if you'll just stand back there, young man, nobody's gonna hurt
you." So I stood back of him while he talked to his prospective holdupee.
The man who was being held up turned out to be quite drunk and
seemed not to understand what the other man was after. Then I realized
that the man with the pistol was also drunk, very drunk.

The two drunks kept talking to each other, the man with the gun saying, "Now I'm telling you, this is a stick-up; I want what you got on you."
And the other man saying, "Well, now, that's not the thing to do, and I
don't have much on me, and what I have on me I need, but I'll split it
with you if you'll just give me a chance and stop arguing with me." It was
actually a very pleasant situation with darkened Cleveland lying all

around, and these two men talking in a really gentle way about their different roles in life, their different means and purposes, and every now and then turning to me and asking wasn't it right what they were saying. I tried to take both sides and still take no side at all, not even my own, whatever it was. After about twenty minutes they got very sentimental and put their arms around each other, and the next thing I knew I had my arms around them and they had their arms around me and everybody had his arms around everybody else and we were singing "Bye-Bye Blackbird" and "Sweet Adeline." We staggered down the street for a couple of blocks and then at a corner under a swinging sign, I excused myself as if from old friends and went on my way.

It was right after this that I walked into the square mentioned in stanza eight. There was a bunch of about twenty or thirty old and young men off to one side of the square. They were being harangued by a man who stood about three feet off the ground in the bowl of what appeared to be an old horse-watering trough. He was saying those things about class struggle, labor bosses, the common man and redistributing the wealth that I'd heard many times before, especially in that now-vanished place called Bughouse Square in Chicago. He must have been about thirty-five or forty and he was doing a very good job. Even though the bowl of the horse trough was no more than four feet across, he actually managed to pace back and forth in it. At the conclusions of many of his sentences he'd stand in the middle of the bowl and hold his arms straight out from his sides in a way that made him look very much like Cimabue's crucified Christ. When he implored his audience to do something about the bad conditions he painted, he would throw his head back and moan straight up into the black sky over Cleveland. He went on and on, and from all evidence he could have gone on forever. A policeman appeared from out of the shadows, walked to the outer edge of the assembled group, listened for a little while, and then sauntered across the square and away into the darkness. I noticed that the men on either side of me were wearing little buttons on their sweaters—the kind of political campaign button that has a stick-pin in the back and can be pinned on anything. The only thing printed on them was a bright red question mark in a black field.

Just before I finally faced the fact that I had better find a place to stay or give up the idea of sleeping at all that night, the man in the horse trough began to accuse his audience of lack of interest in what he was saying, and a lack of responsibility for the world in general. He began to accuse his audience of betraying the working man by not organizing and mounting a revolution against the capitalist system. The old man on my right turned and looked at me as if he expected me to say something. I looked at him blankly for a few seconds and then said, "Sounds easy, doesn't it?"

The old man took hold of my arm and suggested, "Why don't you get up there and tell him off? You can do it, I bet you can; go on, get up there," and he pushed me a little toward the horse trough.

"No," I said. "I think he's doing just fine and besides if we don't like what he's doing, I guess we can just go away."

The old man let go of my arm and sighed, "Maybe we all ought to go away—very, very far away."

And I said, "*Who* knows?"

As I remember, I must have hung around for close to half an hour listening to the man in the horse trough and looking at the men around him. Only the man speaking seemed to have any energy. There was a kind of blankness in the faces, and a heavy sag in the bodies of both the young and the old standing around him. I remember that to me they looked helpless and lost, but at the same time, as if they were engaged in heavy combat down inside. And in the gaps when the speaker paused for a few seconds, a quality of impending vicious destructiveness emanated from the group. It was in those gaps that I half expected them to be joined and transformed in some horrible act of revenge. Not that this mood was entirely strange to me. This was 1933, and there had never been anything at home or in the bank that kept me from knowing what was going on in the streets. I'd been at streetcar strikes in Milwaukee when the scab operators brought the cars out of the barn, and bricks and bullets were fired through the windows. I could remember huge groups of men and women, often with the women in the front, running with clubs and yelling and calling for something that sounded like killing. I'd watched fires outside of factories, and the police running from their over-turned Black Marias. Back on the other side of 1933, us kids who thought we were men used to say "So long" by saying, "I'll see you on the barricades," and as I recall that now I think we at least half believed what our words were saying. So there in Cleveland, that night in 1933, the threat or the promise or the nightmare felt close; and I suppose that is why, among other reasons, such things as "bilious grass," "suicidewalks," ordinary neckties turned into "slipknots" of the hangman's noose and men standing "blank and tense, looking the same, but smelling different / To foxes and everything hunted,"—that that is why these find a place in the poem.

So far as I know the intense frustration and the will to revenge that I sensed in that bunch of men came to nothing, because as I walked away, they were still standing blank and tense, and the man in the horse trough was making words that sounded like a benediction. He, nor anyone else, proved to be their "whippinggoat to flail with a swipple loaded with nails" that night in Cleveland, U.S.A.; all that kind of thing was hap-pening on the other side of the Atlantic Ocean in the world's most liter-ate nation.

Besides the actual and transformed recollections of what happened in that Cleveland square, there was the memory of another event which, in one way or another, fed into these stanzas. This other event, this experi-ence, is tied to the little town of Lemmon on the border between North and South Dakota, between the towns of White Butte and Thunder Hawk, on the edge of the Petrified Forest—in 1937.

It was about an hour after sundown on a cool, windy day in early fall. I was returning from California in a 1934 V-8 Ford convertible, the clear-est evidence I had of having taught two years at Sheboygan High School in Wisconsin. I hardly slowed down for the town of Lemmon, but I did, on the eastern edge of that scattered group of buildings, when I noticed a makeshift carnival operating about two hundred yards off the road. There were some poles against the sky and bare electric light bulbs, not many, strung between. There were a couple of small faded striped tents and some little wooden concessions slapped up on a flat grassless piece of ground and whipped with the dust-laden wind. There were about a dozen automobiles parked around and I parked mine and got out. Five or six kids were riding in tin racing cars attached to a disc, like the floor of a very small merry-go-round that was kept turning by a belt and a power take-off from a very old truck. The engine was loud, and it missed now and then. The disc wobbled its way around, and the kids rode it with blank expressions. Each time a ride was over, one little batch would get off, wait for the disc to start up with another four or five kids, and then just stare at the turning. This was the only ride the carnival offered; the price was five cents.

There were several games of chance, as I remember, five of them. I stood for a while at one of the games. Physically, it consisted of a flat surface about eight-by-eight feet, covered with red oilcloth. Setting close together on this surface was a bunch of prizes. There were little plaster-of-Paris dogs and cats, a bundle of cigars, some boxes with lithographed pictures of mirrors, brushes and combs and the words "Vanity Set," on the outside, and a lot of squat bottles labeled "Perfume." The object of the game was to stand back of a rope, and by tossing the three wooden rings—the kind used to stretch cloth when doing needlework—hope to have at least one of them fall around a prize. I must have stood there for ten or fifteen minutes, and in that time I saw one prize won—a bottle of perfume. I remember becoming quite disturbed by what I thought was a fact: that none of the rings could fit over any of the other objects. For a little while I thought of getting some rings and after throwing them, making a stink about what I saw to be true. But then, as I stood there and watched this go on, I had a very clear feeling that none of this was any of my business.

The five or six men and women running the concessions looked like the saddest sharecroppers ever photographed by the Farm Security Administration. Most of them were blondish, around forty years of age but looking more like sixty. They said almost nothing and they appeared not to see anything they looked at. They collected the rings from the board or from the ground where they'd rolled, and then exchanged them for nickels again. While I was there, there may have been as many as forty people come and go, and in what was a very real way to me, they didn't seem to move as they came and went. No matter what they were doing, they seemed to be standing and waiting for something. They were like people in a stopped movie. They looked like some archaic Greek sculpture but without the smiles that we often find there. They were tattered, earth-colored and quiet in the blowing dust. These were the people I had in mind when in stanza nine of the poem I wrote, "Among them there was a brand of waiting / As if they'd been hurt in the gaps of their reason." These were the people who came back to me when I wrote in stanza ten, "Waiting for waiting, no matter for what." And the "din of the place" that I attribute to Cleveland is more the din of wind, or of an old truck engine spinning expressionless kids in little tin cars and the high whine of a generator keeping two dozen bulbs lighted over a piece of flatland on the edge of a petrified forest.

Back when the new courthouse was built in Milwaukee, the one that still stands there on top of that hill looking toward downtown, there was a lot of talk in the newspapers about fraud. The *Milwaukee Journal* ran a doctored photograph of the new courthouse and it showed the immense block-like structure splitting through the middle and falling to pieces. The article that went with the photograph talked about faulty engineering and hinted at shenanigans pulled off by the contractors and builders. A lot was made of a purported weakness of the foundation of the building. There were predictions that because of the way it was built and the nature of the ground on which it stood, that unless something was done right away, the building would in fact split and fall apart. I remember being mildly worried about this as I looked at the picture and read the accompanying story, but mostly I was excited in a way that made me hope that when and if the building did split and fall down the hill, I would be lucky enough to be there to see it happen.

There was another thing about this new courthouse in Milwaukee. It involved the nature of its design or construction in the huge areas of fenestration. These great multi-floored expanses had been decorated with equally expansive grillworks that proved to be very attractive to Milwaukee's pigeons. Almost as soon as these grillworks were in place, the pigeons began covering them with their gray-white guano. This had been a problem with the old courthouse as well, and to some citizens it appeared that the city fathers, or at least the architects of the new courthouse, had not learned from experience. Interest in the problem was heightened by publication of the fact, or a threatening possibility, that the pigeons were carriers of dangerous disease. All sorts of things were done in an effort to stop the rapidly growing guano deposits. For a while there were special deputies stationed on the ground below the fancy grillworks. They'd wait until hundreds of pigeons were happily perched inside, and then one of the deputies would scare them out with a blast from his shotgun. As soon as the pigeons took wing in the free air above the courthouse, all the other deputies, who'd been at the ready, would let go with their shotguns. They got surprisingly few pigeons, and now and then a sparrow. The fact that they killed a robin one day didn't help matters.

Everything from prayer to poisoning was suggested as the best method for getting rid of the pigeons. One of these methods, which to me as a kid sounded wonderfully original, but which I have since learned is a very old one, called for a tactical emplacement of carved wooden owls about the exterior of the courthouse building. It seems that pigeons do not like owls, and where owls are, pigeons don't go. Owls are hunters and I made use of this in stanza eleven of the poem. In that stanza, I wished to make it clear that even though the man with the word had called it out and that no one had really heard it as a word, still there was some extraordinary response to its vibrations. So what I did was have one of those wooden owls, fixed up with eyes made of mirrors to reflect moving light and objects, respond by trying to hoot. I even had it planted "on a cornice of the courthouse," not just because I knew about wooden owls in connection with the Milwaukee County Courthouse, but because the word "courthouse" should call up notions of law and justice, and I wanted to suggest that law and justice are often deaf to the word.

The five lines of stanza eleven which are concerned with all this read as follows:

One wooden owl with mirror eyes planted
On a cornice of the courthouse
To scare away the chalk-loaded pigeons,
Tried to hoot as the word went out
Unheard, and its flock of echoes bleated away to din and died.

In stanza twelve of the poem, we have the man with the word moving across the country. In those six lines I managed to get him from Cleveland to near Ashtabula in Ohio and then around to New York University.

In a westbound cab driven with abandon
By a moonlighting high school English teacher worried sick
How he'd make ends meet and just barely,
He was carried carrying the word to a bottleneck east of Ashtabula
Where the sign said KNOW YOU TURN and the driver did,
Clear around to N.Y.U.

I don't know why I chose to have the westbound cab driven by a high school English teacher rather than by someone else, or by some high school teacher of mathematics or history or any other subject. However, when I settled on a moonlighting high school English teacher, I was thinking of one very particular high school English teacher who actually did moonlight back in 1935 and 1936. His name was Harry Hydal and he taught down the hall from me at Sheboygan High School. Harry Hydal was about twenty-three, short, fair, and round-faced, the image of a *Verrocchio putto*. I roomed with him my second and last year in Sheboygan in a grand house overlooking Lake Michigan. I'd come home from eating supper along Sheboygan's little main street to find Harry seated on the toilet between our rooms and playing his clarinet. There was something about the sound created in the bathroom when he'd set the two doors just right for baffling the reverberations from the tile walls that charmed him immensely. He'd been first clarinetist and director of the Carleton College symphonic band while he was in school there, and he played magnificently. After a while he'd notice that I'd come home and was listening. "How's this?" he'd call from the toilet, and then he'd go into something he knew I liked. And when he'd finished he'd come out, clean his clarinet, and put it back in the case; "Let's whip out," he'd say.

Harry Hydal, whose old nickname, "Hawk," somehow came with him to Sheboygan, would drive his 1932 Ford coupe around that loop of whorehouses and gambling joints that in those days surrounded the town, and he'd stop where he knew there were slot machines and crap games running. Harry was a phenomenally lucky man. He often took jackpots with a few plays; the dice listened when he talked. Rarely did we return to our place—often at four or five in the morning, with school coming at eight—without his having cleaned up fifty to a couple hundred dollars. And that when our annual salaries were just a bit over a thousand. He was supporting his family back in Minnesota, and he must have figured his nighttime take as regular income. He was, in fact, moonlighting, but never "worried sick / How he'd make ends meet . . ." as I say in the poem. But that was because Harry believed he could sight-read way ahead of what was showing on the drums of the slot machines he was playing, and ahead to the next two upright faces of the dice.

In the poem, my "moonlighting English teacher" is not Hawk Hydal; it's all the other hard-pressed moonlighters who cannot read ahead of the drums, the dice, or time, and who know that for sure.

The "bottleneck east of Ashtabula" in the fourth line of this stanza may go back to a girl named Flossie Wade with whom I danced for an hour one Saturday night in 1943. I'd been driving from Quonset Point, Rhode Island with orders to new duty at Port Hueneme, California, before being shipped overseas. In Ohio I ran into a snowstorm and the going got rough. On the eastern approach to Ashtabula the lights of a big dance hall loomed up. I could hear the band playing country style as I got alongside, so I turned in and parked. I'd driven through from Quonset Point; my legs were a little stiff, and I thought a walk around inside the warm place would do me good—and maybe the snow would let up in an hour or so.

Inside, the dance hall looked like an immense barn decorated with twisted crepe paper streamers. The band was playing "Buffalo Girls," and there was a shortage of men on the floor. I walked around the outer edge of the hall behind a rail, like in a roller skating rink, and then stood at the end near the battery of overhead gas heaters. That's when Flossie Wade appeared, saying, "You're Frank's friend, aren't you?"

And I asked, "Which Frank?"

"I'm Flossie Wade," she said, and after we'd danced for an hour or so, the band stood up and played the national anthem. She said she'd come early, dropped off by a friend going on to some little town to the south, so I offered to take her home. She babbled all the hard-going way through the snow—about her perfect boyfriend who was in Cuba. I dropped her off in the middle of the snow-drifted street in front of the dark clapboard house she pointed out, thirty or forty miles east of Ashtabula.

I made my way around the block and back to what was left of the tracks I'd made just minutes before. It was blowing now. I never made it back to the east-west highway that night. I slept under my navy greatcoat in the car, still a long way east of Ashtabula, snowed-in on the upside of a long U-turn I never intended to make. And the "KNOW YOU TURN" in the next-to-last line of the stanza, comes as one of those things that children and word-minded people find themselves doing: pronouncing single letters as words, like "YOU ESSAY" and "SEE EYE AYE." Here the "KNOW YOU TURN" comes as an entreaty, an urgent request to consciousness of action as it runs.

Stanzas thirteen through sixteen score the academic in macabre images and in terms that have been with me through much of my university education. And, since for a long time in four different universities, I was a student of art history, I settled on "the Institute's early Cinquecentists" to take the brunt—while fleshing out some of my hard-won biases.

The last generation of the Institute's early Cinquecentists was returning
In an Albertian line from a coffee break in step
With footnotes on arches.
They'd given up the trace of man in paint and stone
Along with cigarettes and rhythm-method humanism,
Too troubled on the one hand by the possibility of abscess
Making the heart grow fonder, and on the other
By the harrowing possibility of flat-out confrontation
With the magnificent Italian dead-end.
Ex post facto architectural theory and oldtime unsymbolic logic
Are two slow fasts they kept to avoid the feast of those
They'd slaughtered in themselves.

They walked the radius of a circular park
After carefully stepping over the circumference,
And assembly-lined their way towards the center
Where he who had the word stood,
A physical block.
Knowing that these professing doctors without patience spoke,

And even understood many languages natively,
He pronounced jelly to them in the standard cultivated manners
Of every language, group and sub-family of
Indo-European, Semetic, Finno-Ugric, Dravidian,
Malayo-Polynesian, Turkic, Monogolic, Sino-Tibetan and even
Hokan out of Iroquoian
For that semester's guest in Advanced Etruscan Tub Vaults,
On leave from Princeton and Columbia.
It got into their pores, nostrils and navels,
Their ears, mouths and all aperatures south;
Their teeth, suet, bones and nails,
But it died there, all
Sundered and unheard.

Pushing down the narrow-gauge spasms of their constricted discipline,
They packed up so tight at the compass-pricked center where he stood
That they broke wee puffs of vestigial kamikaze, pre-soured
In the caustic channels of their inner dark.

Outraged by the frustration of their one-track blight-of-way
To the second radius, that if traversed to the circumference
Would give them a whole diameter to their scholarly credit,
They dispatched the most compulsive of the squeezed
Out of the obfuscation to the Bell System to phone
For civil liberties.

Maybe it was foolish for me, a painter from the time I was sixteen, to think that the study of the history of art, under professionals, would answer a lot of the questions my painting was posing for me. Maybe it was just my simple ignorance of the fact that art history, as taught by the predominantly German professors I ran into between 1937 and 1949, was concerned with something that may have been history, but certainly had nothing to do with art. But I went through with the academic program; all the way to the end that came at a sunny five o'clock—after the

dissertation defense and congratulations at the coffee and doughnut ritual—when I walked out of that dark room and rejoined myself in the
open air. Not that it was all that bad, for I'd managed to a remarkable
degree—by short but flashy exhibitions of "brilliance" in a few seminars,
and by merely seeing what was right in front of all of us to see—to dis-
tort the academic program enough to bring it closer to my own shape.

Common among the men under whom I worked in art history was
an occupational incapacity to do their teaching outside of a rather rigid
and easily identifiable system. The core of the system was the one first
published in German about 1915 by Heinrich Wölfflin under the title
Principles of Art History. Wölfflin had recognized, in a great number of
works from the early Renaissance to the late Baroque, certain recurring
characteristics of "form" or "style," each peculiar to the time and place in
which it was produced. To these different characteristics he assigned
descriptive terms such as "linear," "painterly," "clear," and "picturesque."
For Wölfflin, these terms had specific meanings in a developmental type
theory of the history of art. In a word, his *Principles of Art History* holds
that late Medieval and early Renaissance art is "linear," not "painterly,"
that it is "clear" and comparatively speaking, rigid and flat. From that, the
Principles go on in many words and few pictures, to outline a phase-like
development through the Renaissance and Baroque in which the linear
becomes more and more painterly, the clear becomes more obscure, the
rigid and flat become more and more relaxed, flowing and three-dimen-
sional. With Wölfflin's words, and with his selection of illustrations, the
theory works very well. It is convincing enough within the historical
"epochs" he chose to work with.

Wölfflin's' *Principles* represents one of those terribly simple but
beguiling ideas that begs to be much more generative than it deserves—
especially in the hands of persons much less perceptive and much less
intelligent than its founding father. In this respect, Wölfflin's *Principles* is
not so different from the theories of Freud, Marx, Levi Strauss and many
others. So, back in the late thirties and forties, at least, my major professors taught art history in a Wölfflinian box. No matter if the subject was
"Greek Sculpture to the Fourth Century," "American Painting to the

Armory Show," "Northern Painting of the Renaissance," "The Etchings of Rembrandt" or "The Sculpture of Gothic France," it was all Heinrich Wölfflin. All the student was given was thousands of slides with names, dates, sizes, locations and some mixed biographical and bibliographical material—all to be memorized. With the exception of some iconographic nuances to bring to bear, all the student had to do was hang this specialized data on a Wölfflinian scale that ran from clear to obscure, rigid to flamboyant, et cetera, and then he had all that he was intended to get—of both art and history. We wrote papers, of course, but they were meant to exhibit how well we could use the library, cite and footnote sources and avoid being "subjective."

I suppose I could say many of the same sorts of things about courses I'd taken in English literature, history and economics—all with the never-to-be-forgotten exceptions made wonderfully real and valuable by the few great teachers, regardless of the subjects they taught. And, I suppose, this is little more or less than lots of other people besides myself could say about whole passages of their education in academia. But even as I sat in those classes at Wisconsin, Minnesota, Harvard and Ohio State, I was aware of the emptiness that all but the very least sensitive of the professors felt in dealing this way with what they must have known was a great part of the human heritage. Often the semi-darkened lecture halls seemed to fill with moans of their own agonized wrenchings as they read out from their labored notes of denial—denial of the work of art projected on the screen behind them, denial of the life breathing in at least many of us in front of them in the hall, and denial of themselves. I can remember sitting in those twilight halls, my hand working from my eye like a telegrapher's "fist" works from his ear, my mind somehow free to range back to Magnasco's making the original of the counterfeit on the screen, back to the professor's young life in pre-Nazi Germany, or even England, back to my own painting and my own life, and to life all over the world—and I knew that I sat where death dwelt. I wondered how these professors, these men, could go on semester after semester, year after year if not by some mystic and horribly mistaken belief in the rites of their "discipline." I found myself hoping for their own good that in their private lives they were something else, something better, if only alcoholics, snowbirds or flat-out criminals like Jay Gould or even John Dillinger.

In my first year in graduate school I did get some sense of how these men might be surviving as they strangled in "the narrow-gauge spasms of their constricted discipline": by turning the minutiae of art history against itself in games and battles with each other. The playing fields and battlegrounds for these encounters were the professional journals for which they wrote "reviews" of each other's sallies in "Ex post facto architectural (or other) theory and oldtime unsymbolic logic." With these magnificently-honed lethal instruments they went at each other for blood with hopes of killing or at least mutilating. There, in the pages of oversize journals, these dead German professors seemed to come alive as they thrust and parried—their arms and defenses consisting of true or false attributions, correctly or incorrectly quoted documents, postulated monuments, spellings in five or six languages, listings of dates, museums, galleries, stylistic characteristics and *catalogues raisonnés*. There, out of rigor mortis, they snapped up, twisted and jerked in the heat of the crematoria they prepared for their opponents, "my distinguished colleagues." And this they did under smiles, ingratiations and bowings—the civilized manners of the Old World. Linguistic arabesques of timeless wisdom, patience with all the ignorance of the world decorated their camouflaged frustration, never so honestly put forth as on that sign that hung outside the headquarters of C Troop, Second Squadron, Seventeenth Cavalry (Vietnam) showing an angry vulture crouching on a limb and saying, "Patience, my ass! I want to kill something."

I arrived a week ahead of time for that first full year of graduate school and was having a cup of coffee on the lawn back of the Union building when a former classmate from undergraduate days walked up. I'd never been much for Clayton; he'd chased a girl—in his family's Studebaker—who I was interested in during our freshman and sophomore years while I was still commuting between college and the Milwaukee County Home for Dependent Children. I made consistently better time with the girl, perhaps for the simple reason that she just naturally cared less for Clay, but he wondered how I did it. He'd ask me about the shirt I was wearing, or about the one suit I owned—cut down by a matron at the Home from one of the cheap uniform-like suits issued to all the old men in the Milwaukee County Infirmary, up the road from the Home. It didn't fit, and I knew it. It bulged in the middle, bagged in the seat and skimped in the shoulders; the cuff size was out of fashion, it had too many buttons and all the seams were rolled so it looked like a clearly outlined patchwork of armor plate. When Clay asked about it, I told him I had it made—that way. So Clayton Wane took his mother's money and had a suit made like mine. Maybe I should have liked him for doing that, but instead it made me despise him a little more.

"Are you going to be on campus?" Clayton Wane inquired, and I said that I was.

"In what?" he asked, and I answered, "In Art History."

"You're not going to be enrolling in Professor Schwarzkopf's seminar, are you?" he asked, blowing out his cheeks.

"Uh-huh," I grunted. "Why?"

Had Clay smoked cigarettes, he would have reached for one then, but instead he put his left hand, all except the thumb, in the pocket of his jacket and went into a series of shifting contrapostos while staring out over the lake and stroking his chin with his gold-ringed right hand.

He said, "It's tough, Don. It's the real thing, real scholarship. If I were you I'd wait a year before trying it. How's your German?"

"Only Middle High," I replied, "and I can speak and write it fluent-ly—but I can't read it."

But Clayton Wane didn't hear what I said; he never had.

Professor Doctor Oskar Friedrich Schwarzkopf's seminar met in an old room with seats that rose in curved banks around a point dead cen-ter in a mensa on a slightly raised dais. Standing down on the dais that first day, he announced that the subject of the semester's seminar would be "Modern European Sculpture," and that at the next session we should be prepared to let him know on what phase of the subject each of us would prepare his paper. The paper would be delivered with slides, a fully documented presentation of two hours—actually one hour and fifty minutes. There would be two copies of the paper, one to be handed to him to follow as we read from the other. After asking if there were any questions, which there were not, the room went dark and Professor Schwarzkopf gave a two-hour summary of Modern European Sculpture. The slides went through the projectors like shells through a pom-pom gun in perfect timing with whatever he was saying. The last slide, one by Ivan Městrović, slid into place as Professor Schwarzkopf said his last words and the bell rang. The lights came up and he said he'd see us next week. I was impressed with the timing, so exact, like two second-hands on the same clock.

The following week I let Clayton Wane say first what he'd chosen for his subject, and then I settled on one, "Esoteric Sculpture from Rodin to Boccioni," that would give me plenty of room to richly overlap whatever he might say in his formal presentation. Clayton Wane gave his paper three weeks before I gave mine. In those three weeks I worked like a possessed German professor murdering another in the pages of the biggest professional journal.

Once I had the first draft and the slides it was based upon, my roommate at the University Y.M.C.A.—W. Dean Lowry, who was taking an M.A. in Philosophy and who is now a successful insurance adjuster in Illinois—and I ran full-dress night rehearsals for the presentation of the paper. Lowry ran the slide projectors and timed his copy of the lecture. Then, making considerations for an increased rate of delivery due to the excitement the final presentation would engender, the paper was brought to its final form with marginal entries indicating what my watch should be reading as I read down each page. These time calibrations were in units of fifteen seconds. The final night rehearsal was made, Lowry and I horsed around, joked in the empty hall and two days later the paper was given with, by special permission, W. Dean Lowry manning the projectors. I lost about ten seconds in handing Professor Schwarzkopf his copy as I went to the dais and switched on the lectern light. These I knew I could pick up on a long passage on page twelve. The hall lights went off, the projectors shot on and Clayton Wane got murdered for exactly one hour and forty-nine minutes and fifty seconds when, precisely, the bell rang and Lowry flooded the hall with light. The echo of the bell died in the corridor like the "knocking at the south gate" as I came back to reality, gathered up the paper and stepped off the dais.

"Just a minute," Professor Schwarzkopf announced, rising from his seat in the front row and turning to face the group. "I just want to let you know before you're dismissed, that this is the finest seminar report I have heard since 1922." The year on the current calendar was 1938.

"Sixteen years," I whispered to myself.

That seminar paper, my club for Clayton Wane, became by default my master's thesis and put me in line for a Ph.D. fellowship and stipend at the University of Bonn in Germany for the following year. But after the rape of Poland, England declared war on Germany and I heard it come over my car radio outside Waycross, Georgia that September. Someone "up there" must have been watching over me: I never went to school in Germany.

In the poem, as I've said, I lumped all those inhumane academic types—which I caricatured and became in that seminar performance in the species "last generation of the Institute's early Cinquecentists" partly to take a swing at N.Y.U.'s Institute of Fine Arts. For years that art history factory maintained full production under a man who recruited and deployed his art history team with all the skill of a Bear Bryant, and who wrote about Spanish art in a way that read like so many inventory lists. I call them "early Cinquecentists" to put them back in time and to make them specialists in the early sixteenth century—except Mannerist art—in that art so representative of the precarious quasi-classical balance of the Italian Renaissance. I wanted these academics associated with the sterile eclecticism of Raphael's *School of Athens* of 1506, to miss by far the innovative Masaccio and Donatello at one end, and the great rejecter of Renaissance idealistic balance, the late Michelangelo, at the other. I have these "professing doctors without patience" move mechanistically "In an Albertian line" in order to call up the image of fixed time and fixed position, the utterly static character of Alberti's perspective. The geometric symmetry of the professors' "coffee break" choreography should intimate the refined exercises in perspectival diagramming enjoyed during the

Renaissance. Along the lines of such diagramming, I have the professors "assembly-line" their single way towards the center where they run into the man with the word and cannot pass—except for their old gas of suicide: "wee puffs of vestigial kamikaze, pre-soured / In the costic channels of their inner dark." And then, stymied, they respond like many a neo-Fascist, like many an abstractionist who has lost the trace of man and finds he has slaughtered him in himself, they "phone / For civil liberties."

And so, in stanza seventeen of the poem our man with the word is picked up by the police.

The piewagon came full of New York's Finest in new jerseys.
The one with the longevity and double veteran's preference
Invited the word-carrying one inside and he asked why,
Only to be told that it looked like disorderly breach
In a public with no visible means, but
That was a matter for the bench.

The last seven lines of that stanza . . .

When they began to push him in that way
That looks like overly demonstrative brotherly love from the outside,
But feels like valet service mixed with judo and sacked beebees inside,
A small boy with an olive slingshot standing on a hydrant
Said it would be false arrest because
One of the flatfeet was out of uniform, and
Quite suddenly he was released.

. . . refer to a kind of situation more and more of us are becoming accustomed to, even though for a long time it was pretty much reserved for the poor and the different: rough handling by authority.

When I was ten or eleven I used to enjoy standing across the street from the Blatz palm garden at night. In summer the doors were left open and the orchestra music came wafting right over to me. And standing on the base of a fountain, now long gone, it was easy to see deep into the huge darkly wood-paneled room, and watch the "acts" put on by dance teams, jugglers, acrobats, concertina players, magicians and the like. I remember very clearly one night when I was watching from the shadow of the fountain I was grabbed hard in my shoulders and a heavy voice said, "Stealing batteries, eh?" It was a policeman and, with what he said, I was convinced he was going to take me in even though I didn't know what he was talking about. I got a little of that pushing around that looks like one thing from the outside, "But feels like valet service mixed with judo and sacked beebees inside."

Now, my father was a man of average height, average weight, dark hair and shadowed eyes just like most of the descriptions given by never-quite-certain eyewitnesses of the man who did this or that against the law. Because my father kept very irregular hours, was out late at night and early in the morning on foot far from our house, he was often picked up by the police—even when he was stone sober. Twice he was beaten badly by them in sessions my father called "the third degree." He lost most of his front teeth, uppers and lowers—the ones he'd used to open beer bottles—in one of those sessions, and his ribs were broken in another. Then he found out about a charge he could bring against the police: false arrest. I heard a lot about false arrest and settlement damages when I was a little kid.

I was scared, but not quite scared stiff, when the policeman began to handle me there across from the Blatz palm garden. It's mysterious the way policemen and strange dogs can tell if you can't afford a meal or a lawyer; and some of us have had to learn that very early—and we forget it very late, even after we've eaten plenty and have a choice of lawyers on the other end of any phone. But still, that night my voice spoke out and it said, "Officer, I hope you know what FALSE ARREST means." The effect was nothing less than magical. He stopped knocking me around, and after a while in a nice way he asked my name, called me Donald, and said something about the music from the palm garden and didn't I think it was pretty late to be out. I asked him what time it was and offered that I thought I'd better go home—five blocks away.

So, in the poem, a little David-like figure, slingshot and all, stands like sculpture on a pedestal and works his magic again.

Stanza eighteen takes our man with the word into the cotton, oil and cattle country:

Freely bound, then, on his quest for a hearing ear, and giving
To the probability that the word might go forth better inside than out,
He hitched his hopes to a star going west, like
Columbus, but a little more south.
Near the Rio Guadalupe he unhitched and hiked
Through derrick-shaded cotton fields and grasslands studded
With saltlicks and horn-brimmed spectacles
On four legs walking,
Into Victoramus of the Lonesome Star.

"Victoramus of the Lonesome Star" derives from Victoria, Texas, not so very far from where I've lived for the last five decades. I've driven through Victoria lots of times, and I've eaten fried lunches and suppers there, usually near the front glass of a restaurant, and looked out and had all those thoughts about how people make their towns and live in them, and how we hardly ever get to know any place or anybody, really.

I wasn't thinking of Victoria, however, when I wrote in stanza nineteen that the town was "squared off around the courthouse jail." Lockhart, Texas was my source for that, partly because a friend of mine, a British architect named Colin Rowe, lived in Texas for a while and wrote about Lockhart, and how its plan told so much about people's feelings for law and justice, and violence, property, life and time. I don't know if, according to stories I've often heard, there really is an empty

"rose marble room" in a bank in Victoria where cattlemen hunker down
"to trade and borrow / And write notes to the promissory land, but it
always rang likely enough to me, and, imagined, it found its way into
stanzas nineteen through twenty-six:

There on the main street where it most likely would be
In a town squared off around the courthouse jail,
The bank stood looking like a camouflaged safe keeping guard
Over its assorted but negotiable insides.
Through the goldleaf-lettered, plateglass door he went
With an air conditioned by purpose to a rose marble room where
Cattlemen came to trade winds and stock their accounts
While mostly hitting the double-fluted gold bicuspidors.

In the fortune projected beyond Mercator for him, he arrived
To the fanfare of the empty room, and
Took position for unleashing the word
From silence.

While the 33 1/3-r.p.m. platter of recorded electronic bell sounds
Played out the blinded arcades of the phony
Belfry of the Refundamentalistic steeple,
Only to tell time what it already knew,
The cattlemen came dragging their kale behind them.
They hunkered down to trade and borrow
And write notes to the promissory land.
By nicatating and tonguing their cheeks they signaled
The branded hides to change range and hands
Across the taut barbed wire.

Without a sound among the hunkered and one,
Except the almost imperfectible tick
Of the time-lock on the Swiss-movement safe,
And the humming of the cowboy spittoon,

He pealed out the word
Gloriously free in the marble room.
The acoustics were chambered like a nautilus encouraging
The air to perfect vibrations of audible articulations
Corresponding exactly to the letters of the law
And the syllables of the word
Which should have exported the import
Through sensation to the hunkered, but
All that went returned converted to
Unregenerative feedback that bladdered his gall
As memory and not a call.
Undismayed, he mooed and snorted the word, and
Whinneyed and brayed it ass-like around the cattlemen,
All to the same dissolute end.

As on every day in every week, except Sunday when
They played the other game with the lamb,
They went about their silent business in the marble room
As if alone without themselves, unconscious
Of what they did to pay or rob, but doing
It like ritual unconceived, half in dumb neglect
And half in awful vengeance.

The little click that crawled across the wall
Issued from the time-lock pinching tight for overnight,
Signaling the session's end.
Trading their last scents and dollaring up their accounts,
Like sleeves the raveled care,
They amblingly unhunkered for the door.

Once more he intoned the word while the bought sold and slaughtered
Grazed or bled in grass or profusion far from their executors,
Free as stray swine in the county without a hogreeve.
The word splashed jelly on their shirt-fronts, bags of their pants,

Over their naked faces, spread on the ceiling and walls,
Then glacéd the marble floor. Unheard.

Halfway to the filigree porch
He sensed an ideal acoustical balance between spaces
Open and closed like time ajar in the fruit cellar,
And he laid out the word in a horizontal wall
At the level of their departing ears.
It ran around the globe, an earlevel Heaviside layer laving
The pinna, meatus and tympanum,
Then splayed lost in the labyrinth.

The lavish air-conditioned empty room, silent—except for the "imperfectible tick / Of the time-lock" and the sound of spitting men—and lying hidden away from the light of the sun, makes the kind of corner of existence in which monstrous acts are performed so easily because their place of doing is so separate, so insulated from the world they affect. The "rose marble room" is all those penthouses and cellars, forts and mountains, camouflaged railroad cars deep in dark forests, windowless rooms in Manhattan, Washington, Dayton, Prague, Paris, Johannesburg and Moscow. The "rose marble room" stands for the Victory Room with the big maneuvering board, the big put-and-take top, the statistical branding iron that identifies, quantifies and divides men "Across the taut barbed wire; that buys and sells and slaughters them and leaves them to bleed in "profusion far from their executors." And the work of the "rose marble room" is done by men who act as if they are alone, without even the company of themselves, unconscious of what they do, "but doing / It like ritual unconceived, half in dumb neglect / And half in awful vengeance."

———————

For any unheeled romantic who has wandered alone across America, whether thirty or forty years ago or just last month, stanza twenty-seven must sound like the old rhythm of arrival, the hope for only God knows what in the new town underfoot, a half-satisfying disappointment and the moving on out again. You don't have to be "the man with the word" to know about streets paved not only with "dust and darkness," but with longing and divorce; to feel that your unannounced arrival may be met mysteriously by what and by whom you'd always expected but could never name before it and they appeared. Why else did we walk the streets of Delphos, Ohio; Cottonwood, South Dakota; Luisa, Kentucky; New York; New Orleans; Albuquerque; Birmingham; Tulsa; San Francisco; Peoria; Scranton; Chicago; St. Louis; Seattle and all the rest? Why else did we put away a man like Thomas Wolfe, but because he reminded us of our terribly simple dream that the great, good, real and lyrical may lie in wait in the next street or the next town—just up ahead, around that curve? And when we got there we looked in the "lost and found help-wanted personals" and just stood "wistfully, there on the dark corner."

Along the street paved with dust and darkness,
The evening paper came out biased at the seams precisely on time,
And he looked for the lost and found help-wanted personals
In the ads of the have-not.
No one, nor even a tax-whelped corporation,
Syndicate or extremely non-profit foundation garment
For the founder's unction bed was advertising a lust
Or a hunch for hearing.

So, wistfully, there on the dark corner
Where east meets west and north and south to boot,
He watched the kipling down of the town
Into no dreams it had not had.

I once visited the Pioneers' Museum in Tillamook Bay, Oregon:

In the morning,
A little back from Tillamook Bay
Near the pioneers' museum, a child
Playing with a plastic tongue-blade and parts of a pop-up toaster,
Looked his way when he said jelly,
But his mother, harried and wary,
Pulled him back into a narrow coop where
A cock crew and something heavy fell.

And I painted an oil of the coast near Tillamook Bay. It came out a warm sand-colored picture with a great uninterrupted expanse of blue running through the middle. I don't know where that painting ended up—maybe I gave it to someone who liked it but had no money, maybe to Doug Dixon or Ruth Lowman. Anyway, the painting got hold of a lot of what was with me that day along the north Pacific: a quality of intimacy existing almost contradictorily in a wide and deep space; something like what we feel when we look up into a big clear sky and hear the call of a single bird way up there, or like our own voice coming back off the walls of the Grand Canyon.

Tillamook Bay: a good place to have a voice heard, or to have someone turn toward it—a child; a place for a cock to crow, for intimacy to be betrayed.

I've known girls and women who were "certified as mad" like my opal-eyed one in stanza twenty-nine.

One other light of recognition did flicker
In the opal eyes of a girl certified as mad
By a kind of pick-up band acting as a kangaroo court
One night near Natchez when things were dull, and all
The playing cards were stuck together with cruor.
She appeared to hear the word, and weakly
Rasped the dormant nerve a little, just before
Her spoils-system attendant cuffed her far left of crippled
And smothered her under an inner-spring mattress
Behind the tall unwindowed bars.

In my walks from the west end of the Wells-Downer streetcar line, out that mile to the Milwaukee County Home for Dependent Children, more than seventy years ago, I saw and talked to a lot of females certified as insane. They lived at the Milwaukee County Asylums for both the "Curably" and "Incurably" insane. For a period of several weeks, back then, a woman of about thirty used to appear out of a hedge almost every evening I set out on that walk. She'd come at me, harmlessly enough, with the heel of a loaf of rye bread in her hand and ask me to tell her that she wasn't crazy. From the first time she appeared with that request, I obliged. And each time she'd smile, rub the heel of rye bread against my shoulder and walk back through the hedge toward the asylum for the curably insane where, I believe, she stayed.

But the opal-eyed girl of my poem derives from experience with a man, George More, an inmate of the Asylum for the Incurably Insane.

It was spring, April I think, of 1931. I got off the streetcar at the end of the line, had my last cigarette in the car shack and started to the Home. In those days both sides of the Watertown Plank Road stretched out into open rolling fields. The county buildings stood back a good distance nestled among trees. Everything, it seemed, was delicately green; it was about five o'clock, warm and wonderful. And then I heard singing coming from off to the south, from the direction of the Incurably Insane. It was the voice of a man and it was singing "Asleep in the Deep." It was a good voice and would have to be a strong one to carry so clearly the quarter mile across the fields. I followed it to a four-story gray brick building with screened porches across one end.

Stripped to his waist and standing barefoot on a stool, George More was singing out from the fourth-floor porch. He was wearing one of those folded newspaper soldier hats all of us have made, and he was grossly exaggerating a vibrato by shaking his belly with both hands. He carried the song to its end again, holding the last bass note surprisingly long.

"Hello, I've just walked off the cross," he finally greeted, getting down from the stool and showing his hands. "See, they're still bleeding, the bastards." Then smiling very broadly and looking like a photograph I'd seen of Pete de Palma after winning the Indianapolis 500, he held his paper hat over his heart and asked if I was the "Duke of Kackiack."

I said no, that I was just coming from school and heard him singing.

"Then you must be the Duke of Kackiack," he said.

"All right," I agreed. "I'm the Duke then; how are you?"

"The question," George More said, "is how are you, and from here you look like you could stand some learning. You see that shed over there? Well, you go on over there and get those newspapers on the shelf by the wheelbarrows and bring them back here."

The door of the shed was open, and on a wide shelf there were two stacks of newspapers. I took two or three inches off the first stack and carried them back to my place way below George More.

"All *Christian Science Monitors*, right?" he questioned.

"All *Christian Science Monitors*," I replied.

"Now," said George More, "you open up any of those papers and tell me the date and the page and I'll read you it from up here."

"October 14, 1929, page twelve," I called out and he began to "read."

He started at the upper left of the sheet and in a sing-song voice rattled off the whole column, including the texts of the ads below the last article. Then pacing up and down on that high-screened porch, and with the other inmates as heedless of him as only stones could be, he looked out at the sky and kept reciting the exact wordings of the page.

"How about this one?" I asked, holding up another sheet. "August 25, 1930, page sixteen."

After a little pause George More frowned, "Oh, that's the sad one about the woman," and again he rolled off the words as if he had the page before him.

George More asked if I wanted to be the smartest man in the world, and I said why not. He directed me to the general reference room of the Milwaukee Public Library downtown on Grand Avenue, to a particular stack and shelf where I would find a German lexicon. We talked a little more, about tomatoes, as I remember, and I left him singing "Asleep in the Deep."

The German lexicon was where he said it would be, and a few days later I was back on the grass below George More's porch.

"I found the book," I said. "You knew it was there."

"Oh yes," said George More, "and I'd know them all if those telephones would've stopped ringing."

"Telephones?"

He answered, "Yes, the goddamned telephones. They drove me nuts; I told all about it in my book."

"What book?"

"My book. *The Mind that Found Itself.*" He told me where to find it in the Milwaukee Public Library.

The book was there all right, but the author was a man by the name of Clifford Beard. And I read the book; a pretty interesting one about a man who'd gone insane and then came back.

It got to be a habit, stopping to talk with George More. I told my friend, John Mimier, about him and we went together to stand on the grass in the early evening and talk up at that darkening porch. Then, on one of the regular visiting days at the Asylum (George More called it the "Hotel de Rupp" after his doctor) we posed as relatives of his and were allowed to walk with him in a special grassy flower-planted area of the grounds. We waited in the visiting room for him to come down and when he arrived he was carrying a Panama hat.

"See," he said, pointing to his name stamped in gold on the leather sweatband, "I'm your man all right." He was carrying a bundle under one arm and we asked him if he'd brought lunch. "Oh no," he said solemnly. "Much more than that."

For a while we just walked around talking mostly about gardening, and then George More said, "Let's go to the bower over there," pointing to two benches arched over by a white trellis laced with little pink and white flowers. "Sit down," he instructed. "You on that side, and you, brother John, on this side. Now, I know you're wondering what I've got in this bundle. . . . Well, I'm not just going to tell you, I'm going to show you what no other person in this world but me has ever seen."

George More carefully set down the newspaper-wrapped bundle on the grass between where John and I sat facing each other under the arch of flowers. George More got down on his knees, the bundle in front of him, and stroked it. We waited. Then George More began to peel layer after layer of newspaper from the bundle, then one damp cloth after another including pieces of underwear, until the bundle was no bigger than a baseball. He began to tremble a little; his voice lowered. "No other man in the world," he said, and he slowly took away the last wet rags to reveal a peeled hard-boiled egg and some canary feathers which he carefully positioned on either side of the egg.

"See," said George More, "there it is," and he put his finger to his lips. "Shhh . . . and now with the addition of my sperm . . . it will turn into an angel . . . and . . . fly away . . . shhhhh . . . but not quite yet." We stared at the egg, the canary feathers moved the slightest bit in the breeze, and we waited. Then, a little playfully, George More wrapped up the egg and put the bundle under his arm. "Time to preside at my supper upstairs," he said, and the three of us walked back to the visitors' room and returned him to his keepers. "We'll see if old Judas comes by tonight; so long," George More said.

I heard George More sing four times after that; once from his old place on the screened porch, and then three times from a heavily barred window on the same floor. The last time I came to hear him sing there was a rumpus going on in his room, then great cries and figures flashing past the window and George More rushing for the bars and being pulled back, and shrieks and a great gurgling, coughing muffling sound that made his voice sound as if it was coming up from under water or through a mattress. And then it became deathly silent and the light went out.

That was on a Saturday. On Sunday John and I went to visit George More to see what was up. At the desk they told us he wasn't feeling well. And then George More was dead.

I don't know to what voices George More listened, nor do I know what he heard, but my certified opal-eyed girl had to appear to hear "the word" and then rasp "the dormant nerve a little." She had to join the wooden owl and that little kid in Tillamook Bay. And nothing must come of it. So, before we know for sure that she took the word for some kind of reality or not, she was "cuffed far left of crippled," as I figure George More was, and "smothered under an inner-spring mattress / Behind the tall unwindowed bars"—all by a "spoils-system attendant," as I also figure George More was.

Maybe I have my opal-eyed girl in Natchez because of how that name sings against the sound of "mattress." But I knew she must be in Mississippi and couldn't be in Manassa, Aspen, Massilon or Landis.

Mississippi is where a county sheriff told me more than sixty-five years ago, that he'd had to let his black friend be hung because, as a sheriff, he had so many more friends who were white, and the majority rules. Mississippi is where they said, "Why, sure, Yankee, you just go ahead and help yourself," and then punched me in the kidneys when I bent over to get a drink from the fountain outside the filling station. And Mississippi is where that man from south of Osceola picked me up when I was hitchhiking to New Orleans in 1936.

We were rolling along at about forty-five, the black man driving, the fat florid-faced white man on the seat next to him, and me behind on a box in the bed of the Chevrolet pickup when a front tire blew. The white man corked up his pint and the black man brought the truck to a careful stop on the gravel shoulder. The white man called the black man "Camel."

"Camel," he said, "let's get that goddamned wheel changed; we gotta get on down."

"Yes, sir," Camel deferred.

He jacked up the front axle, pried off the hubcap, spun off the five lugs and put them in the open upturned hubcap close to the wheel-less axle. He went around to the back of the truck to get the spare and while he was freeing it from the rack, the white man scooped the lugs from the hubcap and threw them, broadcast fashion, across the road and into a cornfield. He winked at me when Camel rolled the spare into place at the front axle. Camel hoisted the wheel on to the studs and reached into the hubcap. He turned it over and looked around on the ground, then up at his boss.

"Whatsa matter, Camel, you go and lose them lug bolts again?" the white man asked.

"No, sir. I put them right here in the hubcap. Yes, sir—right here in this here hubcap, sir."

"Well, why ain't they there then, you stupid bastard?" the white man demanded. "You better get your black ass shakin' and find them lug bolts, boy—we just ain't got all day, you know."

I started, slowly, to walk away down the road, past the front of the truck.

The white man called out to me, "Where you goin', boy? You come back here. Camel might need all the help he can get."

Afraid to keep going, and afraid to come back, I just stood there. "It's shadier here," I said.

I wanted badly to kill that fat red-faced white man. I could see the headline: HITCHHIKER KILLED IN ROBBERY ATTEMPT—NEGRO HAND WIT-NESS TO FIGHT FOR KNIFE.

I ambled back to the truck.

"These niggers jus' ain't no good," the man railed. "Stupid black sons-a-bitches. Goddammit, Camel! Get them lugbolts!"

Camel kept pretending to look for the lugs. After about fifteen min-utes, the white man said, "Camel, how come you're so stupid you don't know enough to look in that cornfield over there?"

And Camel replied, "Yes, sir. Thank you, sir."

Camel found four of the five lugs, and a while after that I was let free in Jackson. The white man waved. "You be careful now, boy!" he called out the window. "You jus' be mighty careful." I couldn't say a thing. My mouth got full of something sticky and sweet-sour, then like bile, and the busy Jackson street was all blurred and spinning.

———————————

Stanza thirty of the poem goes back to some Saturday afternoons spent on the banks of the Olentangy River just outside of Columbus in Franklin County, Ohio; spent as the poem reads, and sometimes while the Ohio State football team was playing one of its Big Ten opponents during the 1947 season. We have some color photographs taken on one of those afternoons—there are violets in the grass—and even though we've changed somewhat, we have no difficulty recognizing the spot, or each other.

Where the red green and gold lay the deepest along the Olentangy,
Out beyond the beating drum-shaped stadium
And the cemetery begun as a Confederate prison,
He saw two lovers through a sycamore screen.
In the Saturday afternoon sun, with the town siphoned off
Into the billion-dollar football bowl,
They lay there almost alone in Franklin County.
The breeze was from someplace filled
With honeysuckle, frankincense and murmur,
To which they added musk, a trace of fingerling and sighs
They shed their clothes and stabled their cares
And made each in the other's image inseparable,
Wrapped, spathed and spermed anaesthetized.
The moving shadows wrote them in the leaves
And they answered in the last of the sun.
They rose regenerate to a world still at their ease,
And while it held he floated out the word,

Only to pass around and through them;
A light unseen,
A time unkept.

In stanzas thirty-one through thirty-three I'm back in academia with my old biases working against specialists; this time making ridiculous sport of a bibliographer who fails even to sense that "the word" is being called to him, to say nothing of his failure to hear it:

Along his way to the coast
Where the memory of the old oaken Arkies still rapes the path,
He called the word up to a hole in the library facade
Where an Arizona grackle was
Being shot for lunch by a bibliographer.
As the bird fell into the awning below,
The bibliographer leaned out mumbling that:
The first copy, Celery King Collection, acquired from Mogol Flatt,
Is one of six known in original wrappers with all points
Plus inserted four-leaf clover, but reconstructed and
Spine title so pasted that it now heads up.

Just in case the bibliographer was using his mouth to repudiate his ears,
He called the word up the wall between breaths,
Only to have it pushed back with a recitation that:
The Jenny Wren Version is in original condition, possibly
Of black cloth as reported by Heartman and Canny,
And of an issue which,
Like those before and after,

Incorporates some no-name as well as Craghead and Slip titles, and
That if the report is unverified and the variant discovered
Only in green cloth it should be
Reclassified as 3b (issue 3, variant impression 3).

Some swallows homing from Wyoming flew south
While the bibliographer kept spewing his diarrheal down
The classicistic wall by incremental repetition,
And the man with the word walked away west
To the outskirts of Los Angeles.

For the most part these stanzas come, quite directly, from an article
by my close friend and colleague, the distinguished bibliographer,
Professor William B. Todd, formerly of Harvard and for the last several
years of the University of Texas, when he is not at Oxford being their J.
P. R. Lyell Lecturer in Bibliography. I have almost always been charmed
and often disturbed by the lingo of specialists, whether it be that of the
sociologist, psychologist or bibliographer. In some cases, the shorthand
method of exactness employed by specialists merely disturbs me. For
example, the following excerpt from an article entitled "Temptation and
Threat in Nonzero Sum Games," by Philip Worchel, disturbs, but
doesn't charm me.

Assuming equal intervals between treatments, the test for linearity yields an F-ratio of 61.5 indicating a highly significant
trend in the order of defections from Game 1 to Game 5. The
mean square for deviations from linearity, however, results in a
significant F-ratio of 4.48 ($p \leq .01$). The test of the quadratic
component indicates a significant curvature in the trend of the
means (F-ratio of 11.62).

Quite the opposite is true for me in the case of Professor Todd's highly specialized writings. There is some kind of song in that man that must
keep getting sung, or at least hummed back of everything he does. Here

is the section of his article "The Early Issues of Poe's Tales (1845)" which appeared in *The Library Chronicle of the University of Texas,* Volume VII, Number 1, for Fall 1961, that I lifted and bent to my own purposes:

(1a) 1st copy Ellery Queen collection, acquired from L. D. Feldman: one of six known in original wrappers. With all points plus inserted four-leaf catalogue, but reconstructed and spine title so pasted that it now reads up. 2d copy also queen, without wrappers or advts, in modern binding.

(4) J. H. Wrenn collection, lacking advts, in modern binding. In original condition possibly of black cloth D, as reported by Heartman and Canny, and of an issue which, like those before and after, incorporates some N as well as CS titles. If the report is unverified and the variant discovered only in green cloth, it should be reclassified as 3b (issue 3, variant impression 3).

The reference in stanza thirty-one to a road "Where the memory of the old oaken Arkies still rapes the path," is obviously meant to call up U.S. Highway 66 that has one of its ends near the big sculptured lions outside the Chicago Art Institute and the other almost in the Pacific Ocean. It's the highway that many of the Oklahoma "Okies" and the Arkansas "Arkies" traveled west, away from the billions of tons of dust that kept covering their houses and farms in the 1930s. Memories of Steinbeck's *The Grapes of Wrath* get called up, and, for me, thousands of scenes from my own traveling of that road not long after the great exodus. Years ago I began a photographic essay about Highway 66 with the romantic title, "Finger in the Sea." In the poem, I could have had my man with the word travel any road I chose to have him travel; I chose one that I once really knew.

And I had to say the name, "Wyoming," for Wyoming is the name of one of those incomplete and asking moods that still rides with me. I've been there only once, in the summer of 1937, one of those years when the Mormon crickets took over in the west. I worked on the ranch of a man named Charles Starr near Lightning Flat, and in a few days and nights discovered what it must mean for a father and a son and the son's wife to do it all alone in such an expanse. The hard thick reins of the mule-powered hay buck tore my fingers and palms raw before the sun got overhead that first day, and old Charlie Starr could see it would take a long time with me. And I knew I couldn't harden up at his expense; he was paying a dollar a day and the grub stake. On a Thursday I told him I'd better get on my way, that I didn't think I was earning my keep. He was generous, he'd have me stay, but I said I had to go. He told me to wait until Saturday when the mail stage, as he called it, would be coming through, and I could ride with it up to the Montana line. But I left on that Thursday with an unstamped letter in my shirt pocket, written the night before saying to the one back there that I wouldn't be at Lightning Flat any more.

Lightning Flat was a two-story clapboard and tarpaper house, the post office, that's all, and it was ten miles from where I said good-bye to old Charlie and his son. The place was locked and when I knocked a goat clattered down the side steps. And when I knocked again a woman's voice came from up above, "I'll be right down." She opened the door and handed me a dipper of cool water, took the letter from my pocket, put a stamp on it, cancelled it and wouldn't take my three cents. "You're on foot," she said, and I said yes. "Going east?" And I said yes, east. She told me there'd be a Mr. Conway driving to Belle Fourche in a big Diamond-T starting from a crossroads named Forty, thirty-five miles north in Montana, day after next and I could ride with him, she bet. She gave me another dipper of water, a Milky Way candy bar and kissed me good-bye: one of those "swallows homing from Wyoming."

When the great automobile graveyards began to appear all across the country it didn't surprise me. They got bigger faster than I ever thought possible, but their appearance along highways and streets and open fields was like that of an old almost secret friend, but a friend turned giant and mad breaking out into the open for everyone to see and know.

At first, back in the early twenties, dead automobiles were junked with other junk. Sometimes they were rolled into garbage pits along with iceboxes and gas stoves, but usually they were pushed into piles of hard junk, and there weren't many of those. They'd be stripped by scavengers until there wasn't much left but the frame and the central part of the body. Sometimes they were left in backyards, dead-end streets, empty lots and ravines, just like now. But before the massive graveyards appeared, these single stripped cars stood out against the clear-aired scene with a curious and engaging authority like the sculpture of Stankiewicz and Smith. My father's 1918 Model-T Ford came to its end in a weed-covered lot adjoining Weisskopf's garage on Fifth Street in Milwaukee. My brother Fred and I played on it for over two years while it lost its wheels, radiator, seats, steering wheel, lights, rear end, fenders, spare tire rack, motor and finally its transmission box with the three pedals on the side. First it died, and then its eyes, kidneys and heart got used over by someone, someplace. And Fred and I played on the rusting skeleton right up to 1926 when we moved away from near Weisskopf's garage.

It's hard for me to imagine that there ever was a time when most boys, and for that matter girls, didn't go for hunting through, climbing over, sorting out, carrying off and making things out of junk. We were lucky as kids—we almost always lived right next to junk, fine resources of tough wonderment full of actual possibilities. And just like we exhausted our neighborhood library, we exhausted our neighborhood junk. So we took our junk-made coasters to the other branch libraries—heaps and scatterings of junk along the river, railroad sidings, back of warehouses, foundries and loading platforms. We even had a name for what we were doing—"alley hunching," and we were "alley hunchers" bringing back lots of good things. And the day finally came when we got to the "Main Library"—the biggest mountain of junk we'd ever seen, with cranes working overhead and hardly any of it we could lift. It was like coming too early upon the Bibliothéque Nationale, the Library of the British Museum or the Library of Congress. Something about its scale overwhelmed and incapacitated us as ten- and twelve-year-olds. From thinking about making things out of its pieces, we had to shift to an acceptance of an already completed monumental architecture. So then we entered the awful edifice where "the rats peeked out" and old ashen-faced men turned in their rag-filled iron bathtub-beds and cooked on little flames of "Sterno" canned heat wavering through rust-red bedsprings. And then I left it with those with whom I'd found it—boys like Eddie Nolan and his older brother Joe, and Ditz and Dan and a girl like Lillian Johnston. But it got propagated and it poked up all over and spread until now we all look through "the hubcap crusted gate," across "the oiled loam" atrium and into the "bloodpoisonous dark" that is as far from the shadows of my first junkyards as my father's boyhood is from my old age.

What was once an invitation to make, became a cry to destroy, to eradicate. And still the junk jungles grow, environments to themselves; and I have my man with the word forage in one on the outskirts of Los Angeles and find a blacked-out abortion clinic "Operating full-blast in practiced caution."

There, before the expressway begins to be what it expressly is,
He paused at the hubcap crusted gate that gave
To a hundred-acre automotive Forest Lawn.
The sun was burning on the other side of the earth,

Blocked out by the crust, moho and molten core,
But the blackened sky behind the graveyard was caught in the crossfire
Of the Auroras Borealis and Australis and it flickered
Fitfully in a barrage of sheet steel lightning.
The once worshipped graveyard junk gave back
Chromium lights from the bloodpoisonous dark
Hovering close among the grease-cold unhooded heads,
Toothless flywheels flown dead into the back transmission cavity,
Fractured shock-absorbent arms, shocked their last by the lost road,
    hanging
Under the unhinged jaws of girder-booms in once one-piece frames
    and skeletons,
Litters now for exploded doors, undriven shafts, unsteered wheels
    galore;
Universals manifolded, bent twisted, cracked and broken waiting
The clarion call to shrapnel in the next somewhat limited war.
Here and there the angled iron was hung with upholstery crape
    moving
Ominously as Georgia Spanish moss in May
Through flake-edged saws of safety glass.
Between the closed-out open hearses, the oiled loam lay
Strewn with spring leaves and visors for the sun,
Bristling cold with brasted fuel-injection pumps,
Pistons, needle valves, gaskets, shims, handles, hinges
And non-armorial ballbearing escutcheons aping heraldry.

The moon went under and the rats peeked out;
They left their nests in dried-out liquid clutches
And collapsed synthetic seats still half stuffed
With plastic straw and crumbs, to search abroad for sustenance
And openings for fever, tuleramia, typhus, rabies and plague.
To the north an angelus sounded three and three and nine,
Then nine and three and three undoing.

Through the gate he went along the rutted way of delivery and salvage,
Far to the back against a cyclone-fenced hill
Where a blacked-out cut-rate pay-as-you-go abortion clinic was
Operating full-blast in practiced caution.
The German shepherd, asleep full of rats, was chained to a generator
Fitted with an obliterated brand-name in red and fleur-de-lys.
There were little sighs from inside the tin sign lean-to,
And something like ozone from shock treatments in the air.
The television program, on base in the cubical filled with waiting,
Was moving in six near-middle grays
Backed up with muted juke-Bached catechism preludes
While the well-tempered cleaver and absorbent cotton worked
In the padded induction room beyond.

The hidden abortion clinic I once knew of, back in the 1930s, was not in an automobile graveyard but in a large ex-residence on Oneida Street in Milwaukee, and I never got beyond the high-ceilinged, narrow-windowed reception room. But I'd known about the place for a long time and walked past it and wondered how it was that so many could know about the place, standing there in its upright Victorian trappings, and even the doctor's name, and that nothing was done about it.

There was a scent of carnations mixed with the smell of cigar smoke in the heavily-draped reception room. The woman who answered the bell was about sixty, and her vaguely uniform-like dress must have been designed to make strangers think of nurses, or of sympathetic attendants, to go with the very small card that showed through the leaded glass front door: REST HOME. I told her of a problem I said I had, and she began to fill it out for me. We stood near a large oval marble-topped table with black legs, and she kept one hand on it as if she were having her portrait done full-length by someone like Charles Willson Peale. When my eyes left hers to search about the room—over the velvet covered settee, past the stiff Frenchy blue-and-gold chairs facing a fragile table, around to the large blue and white vases that stood on the floor near the portieres to the next room—her eyes followed mine. She said it could all be taken care of for a hundred and twenty-five dollars, but that would depend, of course. I raised my voice in faked surprise and repeated the amount as if I were slowly saying beads. There was something wrong about the woman's jaw, and she sucked at her ill-fitting dentures. I raised my voice still higher. She sucked in the lower part of her cheek and looked toward the door to the next room. I pushed against the marble-topped table with my thigh, a sudden little push, and she jerked her hand up from it as if she was replaying Galvani's experiment with those jerking frog's legs. I straightened up and made an obvious sweep of the room with my eyes. Then very loudly I said, "One hundred and twenty-five dollars, for what?"

It was then that the man in a white barber's coat appeared between the blue and white vases, just inside the portieres. "Mrs. Lewis," he called in a low voice, and the woman turned and followed him as he moved back out of sight into the room beyond.

I stood waiting there in the reception room for a while. Except for footsteps on the floor above, the house fell silent. I wanted to walk across the room and look beyond the portieres, but I didn't. I had the feeling that if I did, something would die and I didn't know what.

No curtains moved in the second story windows as I walked the short path to the pavement and away north on Oneida Street.

All but the mood has changed. Here in London almost forty years later, the pregnant land at Gatwick or Heathrow bound for prearranged legalized abortions in clean professional clinics, the operation to be performed by bona fide surgeons. But the scalper-pimps lurk by their impressive rented cars and make their authoritative talk and herd the nervous to "blacked-out cut-rate pay-as-you-go" abortion racks that keep many a Rolls Royce rolling and many a villa swinging on the Portuguese coast. And the thought is that the drains carry it all away to the sea.

The abortionist of my poem is meant to be more than one who kills by premature delivery of human life: he is also one whose own development has been arrested, whose own life is miscarried and shrinks away. And his life miscarries in a huge theater where life in general miscarries. A theater in which computerized games lay up a projected wasteland as our guarantee of a future; in which suspicion rules more than trust, and fear more than love; a theater in which civilization is so undone that any look is like a vision, a hope, a last straw, as it shrinks away in the train of abstractionist men, gimpy magicians, sick medicine men and its own trailing lust for an atoning violent death.

The abortionist of my poem is the midwife of suicide—his own and ours. And the man with the word calls the word to him; and the man in the barber's coat answers in the only way he wills, by his last and ultimate unfree act. He pushes "the button of his last but one resort," the electrical circuit is completed to the waiting "nine-pound fragmentation bomb" and he and his operation are exploded into incandescence. This is no disguised Christ at Emmaus as Rembrandt drew him, incandescent at the table of the peasants. This is more like me and many of us, who sat at top-secret Electric Coding Machines in the dark off Borneo or Luzon or wherever in that other big war, and knowing where the button was, and the wired bomb, because we-as-the-machine must never be taken, never compromised. The abortionist of my poem is the midwife of suicide— his own and ours; and he knows when the hour has arrived:

> He cast his eyes through a gash in a Clabber Girl sign,
> Past the polyethylene sink to the war-surplus hospital unit inside
> Where the work was being done on an olive drab rack.
> The one in charge in a barber's coat had been a triple-threat man,
> Voted All-American Second Team, the first ever
> From the College of the Maculate on its drive
> To national recognition and fiscal solvency.
> He'd not been good enough for pro-ball, so he'd tried insurance
> Until he heard about visions from the printed testimony
> Of a State's Evidence Witness against a Harvard graduate
> Accused of aiding and abetting the red homonculus.
> Helped by an old head injury inflicted during a homecoming game
>   years before,
> He drank himself to his own sure-fire vision, realized
> In a rebuilt Trailways bus with enormous tent and Hammond organ,

Driven, pitched and played to evilangelize from border to border
    until death
By strangulation of his male organ player cost him all
His new gained wealth, reputation as a healer,
And eight years in the pen.
His pen-pals advised the junk-pusher's trade, but once out,
He turned, rather, to this graveyard procuring of premature delivery.

Now, framed in the gash and obviously at the end of the night's
    agenda,
He was washing and wringing his hands in the sink.
Then, still with the towel, he collapsed
Into the tubular chair at the plastic-topped table and dropped
His head on his folded arms with an agonizing groan.

In the consummate silence that resumed, and musing
How the stars at noon come out from the bottom of the pit,
The man with the word voiced it clearly through the gash in the tin.
It went straight home to the one in the barber's coat
And he rose up in stark naked fright, there
At the end of his camouflaged nightmare.
While his drums still beat with the waves of the word,
And the one who'd given it backed away from the wall,
He reached for the desperate ace in the panic hole
And pushed the button of his last but one resort.

The circuit, by his final unfree act,
Ringed through the trigger to the charge
Of the nine-pound fragmentation bomb,
And for an instant between none and after-image,
Incandescence bloomed in a corner of the graveyard,
Then gave the vacuum back to the rush of darkness
In a rain of junk on junk and rag and bone.

Donald Weismann

Only the rats far out from the epicentrum
Squealed a requiem in life,
And a toad or a dog, someplace,
Strained out an erotic chord.

With the end of the "rain of junk on junk and rag and bone" upon the incinerated automobile graveyard, with that way closed to the word, the man who carries it turns "away from nothing" and out to the open road just as we have done at the close of events that felt terminal.

The one with the word looked away from nothing
Toward the tar-seamed road where the trucks run east,
Lighting the pole-tops and canyon floors
All the winding way to mile-high Denver.

And I chose to have him go a way I know: along the old concrete and black-top cargo routes, watched through tall flat windshields of trucks that whine through the night under the hands of drivers never seen before they stopped and opened the door to let me in.

He pulled over on the gravel and I ran through the taillight-tinted cloud of dust as he swung open the door. It was 1937 and not on the road from Los Angeles to Denver, but on another one that cuts Kansas in half, east to west.

"Where you going?" the driver asked.

"To the coast."

"You live out there?"

I responded, "No, back in Wisconsin."

He had the radio on low, a Cincinnati station, and he hardly talked at all.

"You've got a big one here," I said, referring to the truck.

"Almost empty now; just five left," he replied.

"Five what?"

"Upright pianos. Old ones, reconditioned." He'd started out from Buffalo with a full load and he was selling them in little towns and at farmhouses along the way. "You'd be surprised how many people want a good old upright piano, especially if you can wheel it right up to the front door for them." And a little later, "Music is a wonderful thing."

"It sure is," I agreed.

We rode along, maybe fifty miles, without saying anything. He kept looking at his wristwatch. Then he asked, "What time you got?"

"A quarter to ten."

"That's about right," he said, turning up the radio a little. "I don't suppose you'd think it was funny if all of a sudden I started to sing, would you?"

"Oh no, not at all. I like to sing myself."

"Well this is different," he said. "I have to sing alone."

"That's okay. I don't have much of a voice, anyway."

"Well, you see it's this way: my girl is back in Cincinnati, and when I'm on the road we both listen to the *Cincinnati Hit Parade*. It'll be coming on pretty soon."

"That's nice," I noted.

He explained, "When the program comes on we both know we're listening to the same thing. She's listening up in Cincinnati, and I'm listening wherever I am. I've got a damn good radio; cost me three hundred bucks."

"That's a damn good radio."

"So when the program comes on," he continued, "we both sing and we know we're singing together."

"It's a good idea—both of you singing along with the music like that, together."

"We don't sing along with the radio music. We just start singing our own song right when the program begins."

"It's a fine thing, having your own song, I mean, and singing it like that."

"Yeah," he smiled, "it sure is. Our song is 'The Rosary.'"

"I know that song. I can even play it—not so good, but I can play it on the piano."

When the *Cincinnati Hit Parade* came on, he started to sing and I began to play "The Rosary" on one of the tied-down uprights in the dark back of the van as we sailed across Kansas, away from nothing, it seemed, and toward something still waiting for a name.

"Where you headed?" the man driving the Packard with Georgia plates asked.

"Down south," I said.

"You're there already, son. Where you from?"

"Up north, in Wisconsin, but I've left all that behind."

"You have a good life up there?"

"A lot of people do, I guess," I answered.

"You go to school?"

"Oh yes, lots of schools. I went to six different grade schools. We moved a lot."

"What you going to be when you get through with school?"

"I don't know," I said. "I haven't figured that out yet."

"What do you think I do for a living?"

"Geez," I replied. "I don't know, but I think it must be pretty good."

"I'm the sheriff here."

"I wouldn't have guessed that, but I think that's a good thing to be."

"Young man," he said, looking straight ahead through the dusty windshield, "whatever you do in all your life, I hope you never have to do what I had to do last Thursday."

"If you say so, sir," I agreed.

"You know what I had to do last Thursday?" he asked.

"No, I don't know. I was in Ohio last Thursday."

He looked right at me and spoke. "Son, may God forgive me, but I had to hang a man last Thursday. What do you think of that, son?"

"I don't know. I don't know about it."

"I had to. I'm the sheriff. There wasn't a goddamned thing I could do about it. It was just five miles from here, over there."

"Just five miles," I repeated. "Last Thursday."

"But may God forgive me," the man said. "He was my friend, and may God forgive me, he was a nigger."

The big Diamond-T truck was up at that crossroads just like she said it would be, and Mr. Conway said sure, I could ride on the back to Belle Fourche, being as how I'd talked to the Postmistress of Lightning Flat, and all.

We headed east for a while, in a cool pink-blooming world. I stood behind the cab leaning into the wind, feeling the tears pile up and streak across my temples as the road-riven landscape blurred by. Then the truck slowed down, the air warmed, and the man riding up front with Mr. Conway called out the window that we were turning off to see if "the hermit" wanted anything brought back from Belle Fourche. We bounced through an unmarked gate and twisted and turned in the ruts of a trail that stopped at a windmill. The lower part of the tower was closed in on three sides with stacked wooden beer cases and roofed over with a patched tarpaulin. An old, old man, bearded and bent, stood at the open side.

"Want anything from Belle Fourche?" Mr. Conway asked out his window.

"If you'll stake me, Parley," the old man said, "I sure could use some beer."

"It's yours, Cleet," Mr. Conway agreed, and he turned around the windmill and back across the gumbo to the hardtop.

Still a long way from the South Dakota line, the truck slowed down and then stopped alongside a man carrying a big burlap bag on his back.

"Haven't seen you for a while," Mr. Conway said.

"It's been slow," the very tall, lean man said.

"You've got a full one this time." Mr. Conway noted. "Hop on."

"Thanks, Mr. Conway." The man went on, "The trouble is, though, that it feels heavy as rock all the way to Belle Fourche, but when they put it on the scale and read it off it makes it sound like I was carrying a bag of breeze."

We stood side-by-side, elbows on the roof of the cab, looking straight ahead.

"Sometimes it's a long way to Belle Fourche," he said. "You know Parley?"

"No," I answered, "I've never been around here before."

"You sound like you're from the east. My wife was from back there."

I told him I wasn't really from the east, just Wisconsin, and he said that when you're around Sundance or Forty there's an awful lot that's east, and I agreed.

"You've got a big load," I observed.

"I wish it was a lot bigger. It's wool; I sell it in Belle Fourche."

"You raise sheep?"

"No. I wish I did. I had sheep once, but everything got used up, and in the end she died, anyway—my wife, I mean. No, I haven't got sheep, I just got a little wool—a little today, a little more tomorrow, maybe." And then he told me how it was that he had wool but no sheep: "They're always trying for the grass on the other side of the fence, stretching their necks under those barbs on the low wire and always leaving something behind. So I walk fence. You'd be surprised how much you can pick off those barbs in a mile, two or three. And every now and then, if you live right, you come across a dead one."

In Belle Fourche he asked me to come with him while he sold his wool. He got two and a half dollars for it, and then he wanted me to have a beer with him and I did. And then I bought and he repeated, and all the while he talked of someday getting enough ahead so he could go back to Denver where he'd met his wife, years before, and start all over again.

The man said, "Except for what's hanging on that low wire, there's nothing out here for me."

Each time he said we'd better have another beer—at fifteen cents a glass—I saw another two or three or twenty miles of fence stretching into the distance with little wisps of wool blowing on the barbs, and his fingers, now around the cool glass, carefully picking them off under an immense and empty sky. I spent all but sixty cents of the money I had, and he must have spent more than half his bag of wool. We said so long in the shade under the canopy of the saloon, and he walked west and I walked east. At the corner I turned and looked back. Denver was a million miles that way, at the end of the longest barbed wire fence that ever was, and no matter how hard I strained my eyes along that line I couldn't see a single wisp of wool and not a single dead sheep or a lamb anywhere.

Stanza forty-three gets my man with the word to Denver and the campus of "an accredited university" of the kind we remember as the hibernation caves of the silent generation of the 1950s and very early '60s:

There, after breakfast, he stood on the shoulders of a regential statue,
In situ at the intersection of every concrete path leading
To every clock-wired classroom of an accredited university.
He watched the old children, female and male,
Follow the drawing-board lines like fenced troughs
To their sheep-dip catalogue-described eight o'clock classes.
The deodorized girls were dressed in magazine photographs open
    down the front,
Carrying their transistor books and pancake bags casually
As they walked caressing themselves in nylon sandwiches out of sight
The boys, bereft now of subsidized juvenile delinquency, and adrift
Between recollections of pre-puberty and carte blanche anticipation,
Were thumbing their way to the suck-in of some organizational claque
Where, relieved of responsibility for their acts, should they dare,
Could some day soon dandle the oscillations of their erotomania
On an expense account while doing what's necessary only
To provide statistics in support of a long deceased fiction.

At the end of World War II, and while still on terminal leave in the uniform of a junior grade navy lieutenant, I went back to look at the college from which I'd been on military leave for the past three years. I'd already been to Milwaukee to see my father, whose life I'd come to graceful terms with during my time in the South Pacific. I must have wanted to make this clear to him in some better way than just telling him that now I really did understand and that everything was okay with me. I took him to a baseball game, the Milwaukee Brewers versus the Toledo Mudhens, and I carried a case of cold Schlitz to the best seats in the grandstand. For a while it felt like going back to 707 Chambers Street, back to the early twenties and Sundays on the porch listening to the Brewers play and watching and hoping for another foul ball to bounce fairly into our hands. It felt like an unwinding back to a place and time before we'd lost each other; soon the old road, lost at the fork twenty-five years before, would appear and we could travel it as if the time between then and this summer afternoon of 1946 had never happened. We'd come early to the ballpark, but what I didn't know was that an exhibition by the "Hell Drivers" was scheduled before the game. The cars were revving up before we'd finished our first bottle of beer. The helmeted, white-uniformed drivers waved to the stands and for the next thirty minutes the outfield was a montage of leaping, rolling, crashing and burning automobiles. When one of the drivers ran limping from the flames of his capsized car, my father said, "By God, Donny, that's the way to live!" The Brewers lost in a long drawn-out game, and a lot more than half the case of Schlitz was left for the scavengers.

I bought a 1931 Model-A Ford coupe in Milwaukee and drove down to Normal, to the Illinois State Normal University where I'd been teaching before the war, as I've said. I wasn't sure that I'd ever go back to teaching, but I had to look at the place again, walk in the halls, hear the voices coming out of the classrooms, stand where I used to stand before I learned for sure that death was the one guarantee of life, and talk to whoever I used to know before the war. I expected a lot of change; besides VJ Day and VE Day there'd be some deeper signs of victory, some hard evidence of trying to do better with life. I expected that the returned veterans, maybe especially the early returned casualties, like the ones we'd transferred by the score from the burned *Princeton* almost two years before, would already be making the new case, but maybe it was too early.

In the hall of "Old Main" I saw the dean. At first he didn't recognize me, but then, with help, he did, and we stood at the newel post by the stairs to the second floor and talked for a few minutes—about enrollment and budget problems. I stopped by the president's office and asked the girl if he was in. He was. He asked what I'd been doing in the navy; I told him and it disturbed him. He told me how difficult it was going to be for veterans like me to return to teaching "youngsters," adjusting, and not letting our war experiences affect what we did in the classroom. Still, he wanted to hear that I'd killed some "Japs," and so I told him, and even after he got red in the face and started to shake I kept telling him—stories of our boys making sure by keeping the .50 calibers on them until they were ripped to shreds on the parachutes and there wasn't enough weight left to keep the umbrella open; and commands like, "Mess boys take over; strafe survivors," after the pig boat was hit and going down.

"But, President Fairchild," I said as I got sicker inside, "isn't it great to know that we all worked together to win; you here, holding the fort, as it were, and us younger ones out there doing our part?"

And all President Fairchild did was shake and finally say he was glad I was back.

But I still wasn't back, and I knew it. I spent that semester in Mexico and taught the following year there in Normal, Illinois. After that it was Ohio State, a Ph.D., and teaching at Wayne State University in Detroit and by that time it was 1950, five years after MacArthur and the Japanese had met on the battleship *Missouri* in Tokyo Bay and World War II was over. Even with some kinds of new language, words at least, and the ending of one part of my life in a going-away bonfire of memento mori and the unreality of a legal divorce. nothing seemed to have changed much. The veterans who'd come back in droves and went to college under the G.I. Bill opted for reading and a chance to get ahead in the world as it was, "To provide statistics in support of a long deceased fiction," and I was one of them. Once time had stretched a veil over the sharp outlines of the maimed and the dead, and over the smallest vignettes of horror— like the puppy playing up front in the PV-2 while we strafed a bus full of people on the island of Truk—once most of that faded into impossibility, it was pretty nice again with the grass freshly mowed, the sky fleece-wisped and spring come back:

The grass had been cut and rolled by tandem power mowers,
The brick and stone courses tuck-pointed that spring;
The windows were washed and shaded adroitly with pastel blinds,
All under a fleece-wisped sky so deep and high
It took more than the naked eye to find the vapor streaming
Behind the military budget, just before the sonic booms.

Memory is as self-protective as the chameleon's skin, and it covers the body no less. It changes or fades away in the face of overwhelming threat and shows only what will make it unseen. Its billion sensors pick up the clues to survival and cut off those that would cripple and kill. And in the 1950s, even with the afterimage and echo of World War II spread across Korea, millions of veteran memories survived in protective coloration and selective hearing. The tolling of the word, though of earthquake force, was not heard; it "lay on the land / Like the sound of a bell made of meat."

From this high place of vantage, straddling the close-spaced ears
Of the regent unremembered though cast in bronze way before the
    day he died,
The one with the word filled his lungs with the colloquial
Air of the place and broke forth the word through the unexpecting
    hum.
Its crested waves were seismographic and little inked needles around
    the world
Charted the duo-syllable jelly, just so, on paper rolls and drums.
But its sound, if to them at all, lay on the land
Like the sound of a bell made of meat.

In the poem I was thinking of something like the heavily-cushioned sound to which I awakened that warm spring night in Detroit in 1950. The light gauze curtains at the bedroom window facing Third Avenue were blowing a little. It was a little after three, time for hearing Detroit's gaudy hot-rodders racing through the deserted streets. But then I remembered that that sound had all but stopped a couple of weeks before, right after the police hired a dozen racecar drivers and put them behind the wheels of powerfully souped-up unmarked Mercury sedans. For a while I'd hear the single hot rod barreling wide open down Third Avenue, and then the Mercury hot behind. I used to lie and listen to the chase, the fiery sound of the straight pipes, the screech of tires rolling and smoking in the turns, the going away and coming back through the slum around Wayne State and often, blocks and blocks away, the final sound of the crash against a pole or wall, then silence, and soon the sirens coming up to a radio call. But that was over, for more than a week. This was something else—less sharp, less clean, mushy and ominous.

I went to the window and leaned out. Along Third Avenue as far as I could see there was lumbering out of the darkness toward me an unbroken column of heavy rubber-treaded tanks. The olive drab top hatches were open and from each a man, visible to the waist, leaned forward. One of them looked up as he went under my window. He must have been about twenty. The old building trembled and I heard the two maiden ladies moving about in the apartment below. They came rushing up the stairs and knocked at the door. I let them in and they asked if America was being invaded. They blurted out about Belgrade in 1941 when the Nazis came and how they didn't know what to do, and how they pulled down the shades as the tanks went by. Trembling, they asked where they could go, and I said that everything would be all right; the tanks were ours, coming, maybe, from the Cadillac plant where they're made, and being delivered, perhaps, to someplace like Korea. We stood at the window, shade up, until the last one and a trailing Jeep were out of sight in the direction of the docks along the Detroit River. But the deadened rumble of their passage lay in the street like a mushy black pavement until dawn and the first light began playing tricks with memory.

And so the returned veterans melted chameleon-like into the silent younger generation of the 1950s, and I, as one of them, taught an only slightly skewed brand of the history and criticism of art in three state universities. We couldn't play the games of my poem's "paranoiac dean" any more than we could play with power based and engendered in fear, with the falsification and forgery of documents, with lies, electronic snooping, the interception of mail, blackmail and character assassination—the new legacies of "Tail-Gunner Joe" McCarthy, the fake hero-veteran who showed a short TV generation how to suicide by killing others.

For years the university campus played dead at "bingo-jargon games" full of instant clichés and intellectual chic, at crises concerned with where upperclassmen should park their sport cars and at tables full of charts showing how much a Baccalaureate in Engineering was worth in the sellers' market compared to one in Classics, Philosophy or Physics. The Greeks played on their aphrodisiac lawns after dinner, the stadium was full every Saturday and prizes were given for fitting snugly in square holes no matter the shape of the plug, while "the vines quietly clawed their way up the wall," and, not quite unknown, some few students were "plotting toward truthfulness," no matter how blindly, how romantically ideal.

So, in the poem—with reference to lost time and to the 98th meridian that cuts the globe just west of Austin, Texas—I say:

With no more adieu than the day is lost going west
Across the line on the other side of the Great Plains beginning,
They went their sequestered ways, some to bingo-jargon games
    played with ponies
And some few to non-sequiturial lectures full of perspectives by
    incongruity.
At ten minutes to nine precisely, and by a Pavlov bell multiplied,
They made the doors and steps back to the concrete belts, and on
To the half-circle clearing under the Tudor windows of the Vice
    President
Where they demonstrated, minuet-like, about certain campus parking
    restrictions.

The mousey faculty judges, appointed by the paranoiac dean,
Sat after an engraving of Raphael's *Disputa* on a balcony hung over
The exactly prescribed student demonstration area,

Donald Weismann

To score by points on square tagboard grids, easily fitted to the lap,
The comparative degrees of decorum as defined
In the regentially prepared and newly re-tied Hand and Foot Book
    for Students;
And as manifested by the various Greek letter groups
Of the Pan-Hellenic Society during this particular demonstration
Now ending on time, four minutes before nine.

The winning group, a sorority whose strategy had been passive
    assistance,
Was present only by proxy in the person of the sorority father, who
Happened, also, to be the paranoiac dean.
He was outrageously applauded by his self-appointed judges
As they presented to every member of the sorority, in absentia,
A gold-stamped, top-grained cowhide slip-on cover
For their personal prints of the Hand and Foot Book.
After the Pan-Hellenic hymn was sung, and a maintenance man on
    the roof
Ran the Decorum Flag up to the soft underside of Old Glory,
The President of the Senior Class led them in collective unconscious
    meditation,
While the vines quietly clawed their way up the wall.

From his perch on the dead regent's bronze pate,
In the still of twenty-seven seconds to nine,
The man with the word loosed it loud again and then attended
The echo's funeral procession all along the ring around
The Rockies' pocket full of mile-high Denver.

Somewhere in cellars or bunkers far back and under,
Some other students may have been plotting toward truthfulness,
But their retreats kept out as well as in,
So what they did and said was as dead without
As jelly was within.

Stanza fifty-one takes the man with the word to an army camp:

Over a ridge where a path falls down in Maryland,
The man with the word angled his way to Camp Pinkerton,
Named for Allan the cooper who foiled the Molly Maguires, and
Kept Old Abe from being shot until Booth did it in a box
And Allan's sons went a-scabbing in May with labor spies.

The camp could have been located anywhere and called by any name. I settled for a giant step from "mile-high Denver" to "where a path falls down in Maryland." And there, with an expanse of America behind, I named the camp "Pinkerton" to care for my childhood romance with stories of the Scottish barrelmaker who caught counterfeiters and became a sheriff, then Chicago's first city detective almost a dozen years before the Civil War, and foiled the plot to assassinate Lincoln on his way to the 1861 inauguration. But the Pinkerton story, of which I am still reminded whenever I see those nicely colored embossed signs on glove cases saying "Protected by Pinkertons," is shot through with all sorts of cross-purposes and ambiguous loyalties that are distinguishable only in relation to a shifty opportunism and the convulsive fits of nineteenth-century industrialism. Allan Pinkerton—who did everything from operating a station on the Underground Railroad to hiring Irish spies to get the goods against the organizers of Pennsylvania coal miners and have twenty of them (the Molly Maguires) hung—left his National Detective Agency to his sons, Robert and William, and they made it a more frankly C.I.A.-type espionage outfit serving the "Robber Barons."

Donald Weismann

Something about this ragged piece of Americana that touched my life through confusion with stories of Nick Carter and Sherlock Holmes, felt like the right kind of rickety bridge into an army base:

The pup and top-dog tents were neat in row on row,
(Oh gently down the scream with a PX whisky wash),
Well away from the officers' mansions covered
With masonry hors d'oeuvres and rank flags flying
In the slipstream of another smokescreen investigation,
Involving low candlepower in the mess hall and shower,
Trumped up to wet-blanket the red-hot charges
Of brutality to the literates refusing to use in time of peace
The toilet articles of war.

Stanza fifty-three caricatures something of the military, political, technological and human grotesquery that the war in Indochina may yet serve to make clear is the norm for every war.

Hard by the electric picket fence, where
A sign shouted out PEACE IS OUR PROFESSION—SLEEP WELL TONIGHT,
The motor pool stood shimmering with rockets
Rigged up as bookmobiles and ambulances.
The half-track bicycles, bought on a southern contract just before
    election,
Were lined up smart before the amphibious baby carriages
Loaded with gesundheit bazookas and four-in-hand grenades.
The high flung command cars with mohair seats were back
From a Colonel-and-up safari in New Nations Africa,
With side trips to the Western Indies and ex-French Asia,
And they lined the mall through the center of the pool
Draped with trophies and form letters from off-Central Intelligence.
Between the ram-jam radiation bulldozers, uncontaminated earth
    spreaders,
Troop-dropping trucks and mobile missile planters, a Private First
    Class
Was reaming the tail-pipes free of carbon vacuously
When the man with the word hissed jelly through the fence.
The Private kept reaming as if dreaming of the metaphors
He was mixing, and pointed blank to the mess hall yonder.

I never was in the army, but before I volunteered for service in the navy in 1943, I was a civilian specialist with the Army Air Forces Technical Training Command. I taught radiomen gunners the International Morse Code and procedures for radio, radiotelephone and visual communications. That experience, which included going to the University of St. Louis for training and then teaching enlisted men in Chicago, gave me my first feelings for the growing military-industrial monster that always seemed to be on the verge of going completely out of control, of going off on its own like one of those "things" or diseases in early science fiction.

Early in 1943, while I was teaching at the Illinois State University, I heard a Major Fischer make a speech about how badly the Army Air Force needed teachers of radio communications. I knew a little about radio, mostly from my older brother Fred, who years before, had built the first crystal set in our neighborhood. So I got the information from Major Fischer and went to St. Louis as a member of the seventh class of radio operator trainees. Living in a dark, cockroach-infested pair of rooms on Sarah Street, I went to school eight hours a day and three at night, six days a week for seven weeks. In the run-down rooms of the University of St. Louis, I sat through classes in Alternating Current, Vacuum Tubes, Communications Equipment, Radionets, Communications Procedures, Radio Telephone, Visual Signaling and International Morse Code. With the exception of the course in vacuum tubes, the curriculum was taught by bored men who mumbled material that, when it could be heard beyond the first few rows of the room, sounded like noises from a dying train caller reading from an electronics supply catalogue. Cheating on the examinations was so widespread it appeared total. Some of the class always had the answers almost as soon as the exam was begun and they were passed along the rows as if that was part of the regular procedure.

Teaching and learning the code was something else. For a few hours each day we sat in classrooms wired for sending and receiving audio International Morse Code. The instructors, ex-radio hams and ex-merchant marine radio operators for the most part, sat up front and hand-sent the code to us at our positions at long tables. Working from master copies of five-letter coded groups (KBNOS OWERT CDRMP, etc.), the instructor would send for five or ten or fifteen minutes at a given speed and then have our copies checked against the master. In the seven weeks I spent in St. Louis that winter, I managed to achieve only twelve words a minute; sixteen were required for graduation.

The night before the last day of classes, class RO-7 threw a party at a nearby hotel. Several of the instructors came, including my code teacher, an ex-merchant marine radioman of about fifty. The party was simply a means for everyone to get drunk together inside the protective walls of the hotel. Around ten o'clock I went to the men's room. My code teacher, really a pretty good guy, was lying stretched out on the floor with his head in the urinal, very drunk and fast asleep. I got down and called his name; I shook him. He was like a corpse, but breathing. I didn't want to leave him lying there, so I muscled him around and over my shoulder in the fireman's lift and began carrying him out when he started to talk, his head hanging down behind my back. He recited some unidentifiable verse and then asked who I was and where we were going. I said I'd get him to a bed in the hotel, or home, if he wished. Then there followed all those air-drawn arabesques and recitations I remembered from the old days with my father and his pals, Johnny Otzelburger, Soapy Wallace, Ed Wink and dozens more, and after a long time we were out in the street with no taxi wanting to stop for what must have looked like bad news. In the end, I carried my code teacher all the way to his apartment on the fourth floor of a gray building near the university. I put him to bed, had a last whisky with him, and he thanked me, using my full name.

The next afternoon, the last day for class RO-7, the code teacher—seated behind sunglasses—called for a final code check at sixteen words a minute. I tried so hard on that test that part of me seemed to die. It was obvious halfway through that I'd failed: my copy was full of holes—whole coded groups I'd missed. But I went on to the end like a spent bullet that had missed its target. When the teacher called for the papers, I didn't hand mine in. He riffled through the stack and then called out, "Weismann, where's your paper?" and I passed it forward.

A little later he called out the names of those who'd done a "solid sixteen," and my name was with them. It was a lie and a thank you bundled in one, and I decided I'd accept it, gratefully. I figured that when I'd start to teach I'd be able enough all the way to twelve words a minute, and that in the time it would take me to get my first group of radiomen gunners from zero to twelve, I'd have gotten myself to sixteen. So I graduated with the class of RO-7 and reported in for teaching at the Stevens Hotel on Michigan Avenue in Chicago. It turned out that most of that huge hotel had been turned into a barracks; the teaching was being done in the old coliseum on State Street, the very place where William Jennings Bryan had delivered his famous "Cross of Gold" speech at the Democratic national convention in 1896, two years before Captain Sigsbee lost the battleship *Maine* in Havana harbor and forty-seven years before I arrived at the front door with class RO-7.

An immaculately uniformed master sergeant with a huge barrel chest and a sharpshooter's medal pinned on his blouse came out of the room labeled STAFF and asked, "All present?" and no one answered.

"Right in here and sit down," he said, mostly through his broad nose that appeared to have been broken more than once. "First, let's get this straight: you're not liked in here for the simple reason that you're civilians. We're using you because we got nobody else right now. And you're going to be teaching soldiers, the men who are fighting this war for you. And you better remember one thing: you better not make any mistakes because the ghosts of those soldiers you kill will be back to bother the hell out of you for the rest of your life. Okay. Code check in the next room— that way. Let's see if you've learned anything."

We sat down at tables equipped for sending and receiving. "I'll tell you when to put the cans on," the sergeant said. "And keep your hands off those keys. Your code will come off the best punched tapes in the world—no excuse; I'll feed you one minute at four words a minute and at eight; five minutes at twelve, five at sixteen and five at twenty—and you better have twenty a minute every minute if you expect to do sixteen with those soldiers. Okay, put the cans on, here it comes."

I passed four words a minute as my world blew away and I failed, full of holes, at eight. The sergeant looked at me as if I was a dog turd he'd stepped into with his brilliantly shined shoes.

"What the hell's with you?" he asked.

"Nervous, I guess."

"Those sons-a-bitches in St. Louis don't know their ass. Get in there and for Chrissakes listen to code. We'll check you out tomorrow, and I do mean out, at sixteen hundred—four o'clock to you," he said.

At four o'clock the next afternoon I flunked eight words a minute on a check run by one of the civilian supervisors, a man named Petkov. I told him I thought it was hopeless, that I'd better just resign and think about what I should do next.

"Don't take it so hard," Petkov said. "You think too much. Taking code is just an ear on the end of a pencil, no brain between."

"Maybe, but I better shove off."

"Hell, you leave now and you create all kinds of bookkeeping problems, and this place is all snafued anyway. Stick around; you got thirteen days 'til pay day. You can sit in here where it's nice and warm and listen to code if you want to, figure out what you're going to do next, and then take the dough and do what you're going to do."

"You know," I said, "I just might do that."

And I did. I figured I couldn't go back to my teaching job, and besides after that farewell party they'd given me when they all said how great I was for leaving a good job with a deferment coming up and a "C" gasoline sticker, just to serve my country—after all that, I couldn't go near Normal, Illinois. So, as the bitter cold days whistled and moaned outside, I sat in the warm little code room, earphones at my temples, deciding what I'd do next. I'd gotten pretty sick of being looked at as if I was a scabby naked man as I went back and forth on crowded streetcars still in the clothes of a young assistant professor of art—and I figured I'd enlist in the navy, but first I'd get some money, for what, I've forgotten. So, it finally got settled in me: I'd drive a cab for a few weeks—I knew

Chicago pretty well—and get four or five hundred dollars ahead and then see about the navy. Once this was settled, a fine feeling of freedom took over. I came to the code room when I felt like it. I walked around Chicago, saw a lot of movies, watched the ice pile up along the lakeshore, sat for hours in front of my old favorites in the Chicago Art Institute and wandered freely about the huge coliseum with a marvelous sense of detachment.

It was around five o'clock one evening that this detachment, this feeling of freedom, was thrown back into jeopardy. I was walking along a kind of catwalk that ran around the interior of the building, high up three of its walls. From there I could see, almost at once, the entire expanse of the concrete floor below. I thought of Bryan at the convention, the thousands of people and the noise that thundered at the ringing close of his speech that said man would not be crucified on a cross of gold. I thought of the great prizefights that had been fought to the last bell in a ring in the center of that very floor way down below the dust and soot-blackened banks of megaphones, and a string of names I'd first heard from my father—Joe Gans, Battling Nelson, Harry Greb, Benny Leonard—came singing back to me. But the great hall was all but silent now. Only a very hushed stirring mixed with the distant hum of the glassed-in automatic tape machines held off absolute quiet.

Yet down there, spread across that floor, close to two thousand men sat taking code in walled-in unroofed plywood cubicles. It was like looking into a huge egg crate, each square filled with khaki-colored shapes that moved a little now and then. And for the two thousand that sat down there now, there was another two thousand back at the Stevens Hotel that would be coming into the crate at eight that evening, and still another two thousand after that. Six thousand men came into and went out of this crate every day, carrying battle gear to get them accustomed to the weight and to the changing shapes of their bodies.

What suddenly got to me as I stood there on that catwalk was the fact that whether or not I left this scene of the Army Air Force Technical Training Command, I was already packed into the crate that extended far beyond the walls of the coliseum outward across the country and into the whole warring world. And then a voice cracked out over a powerful electrical system and hit the still air of the coliseum with a directive from the commanding officer. The total unified effect of that voice on the men below gave me a deep and lasting chill. It was like nothing I'd witnessed before, nothing: two thousand men sat bolt upright and remained motionless until the words "That is all" came over and then, as man, they bent back to their work. Something of this quality of total and undifferentiated compliant response is what I meant to get into stanza fifty-four of the poem. There I have a colonel "cue-in the command that wracked the hall in tiers of attention," and I have the man with the word try to appropriate the silence for the sounding and hearing of the word.

The siren way up the water tower bewailed the loss of morning,
And half a division of non-commissioned flowers of youth
Anthologized at the steam tables of their mid-day meal.
At the decibel height of the uncushioned mess hall clatter,
When seven and half thousand were in a single sight,
The cocky chicken-Colonel appeared in starch and brass at the open
    front door,
Flanked by two West-Pointed Majors and a pair of VMI Captains to
    keep the score,
He cued-in the command that wracked the hall in tiers of attention
And laid away the last living sound in the fresh-created mausoleum.
Into this erectilinear solid of silence, and before the next regular
    command,
The man with the word sent it forth in a blast of sound that
    resounded
From every atom in every molecule of solid, liquid and gas.
But the half-division of men with a full division of ears
Stood as a single frozen stone,
Numbed deeper into dumbness by blind respect and fear
Of the uniformed team-shaped myth, mythically champing at a
    glorious bit.

My time as a civilian specialist in communications was running out in Chicago. The day before payday Petkov came into the code room and sat down at the far end of the table.

"What you going to do?" he asked.

"Drive a cab for a while and then join the navy," I said.

"And see what's left of the world," he said, and I said I supposed so.

"Put the cans on," Petkov said, "for old times sake."

So I put them on and as the code began to run I started to letter in the special way we'd been taught—so that the end stroke of every preceding letter left off in the most advantageous position for the starting stroke of the next. My mind was off reading a map of Chicago, the streets and neighborhoods I didn't know about, getting ready to drive a cab. My hand kept making letters on the page in front of me, and I watched the neat five-letter coded groups grow in lines across it. It was like absentmindedly watching a fast moving hand-shaped machine out there on the table all by itself. Then my own hand became very tired. My fingers stiffened up and I couldn't make them move.

"Let's see those sheets," Petkov said, dropping his earphones and coming quickly up to my end of the table. He laid my sheets next to the master, checked the last two, and then, half smiling, he said, "These last two sheets are solid right."

"The hell you say," I exclaimed.

"Do you know how fast that last tape was?" he asked.

"I have no idea,"

"Weismann, you old malingerer," Petkov said. "You just copied a hundred groups solid at thirty a minute; on a typewriter I'll bet you could do fifty."

I went to work the following week, on the midnight to eight shift, seated at a control panel called a BD 157 with my first class of eighteen radiomen-gunners, nine on each side of me down a long table. Within the week the master sergeant with the big barrel chest appeared at my control panel.

"How the hell did you get here?" he demanded.

"Sergeant," I said, "I'm just getting to know these soldiers and they got a saying I don't understand."

"What's that?"

"Fuck you," I said.

With that open invitation, the sergeant came by every night and unloaded tons of invective on me. And although I figure he made colonel in the years ahead and was finally fragged in Vietnam, still he provided me relief from the most boring job I've ever done with success.

And then one day I walked into the office of the navy's officer procurement division in Chicago, answered questions, tried to hide the fact that I'd ever done anything in radio communications, took the physical exam during which a lieutenant M.D. told me my ears were dirty, and was told to go home and wait to hear from them.

I was created an ensign by a phone call from the Chicago office and told to read the *U.S. Navy Regulations,* a copy of which was in the mail to me, buy uniforms and report to the Navy Training School for Communications at Harvard University. I was much taken by a piece of advice in the *Regulations:* Always have plenty of maps with you; you never know where you'll be going. I worked hard at Harvard and was selected for an extra month of super training as an aircraft carrier communications officer and then was shipped to Port Hueneme, California for training with the marines as an amphibious communications officer. The *Articles of War* were finally read to me and four other officers aboard a merchant ship, the SS *John Shafroth,* as we sailed south of Samoa loaded with gear for amphibious landing. By blinker in the black of night somewhere in the area of the Admiralty Islands, we rendezvoused with the rest of our outfit, destined, according to orders, for a place with the code name "OUCH." The commanding officer of our outfit, a three-striper from St. Louis, came aboard and told us to sit down. "I've got news for you," he said, "I've made the circuit out here, and I want you to know that we'd better hope to God that the enemy is more fucked-up than we are, or we're going to lose this war."

And so the enemy must have been, all the way I went, through New Guinea to the Philippines. Stanza fifty-three, though concerned with another war, carries something of the ceremonially mad character of what I experienced as war in the South Pacific in the 1940s. To me, it amounted to a gigantic stage production of a skewed Brechtian tragedy interspersed with long soliloquies from fairy tales and *Joe Miller's Joke Book*, butcher shop scenes run on revolving movie screens, unchoreographed Byzantine dances performed in the wings by the brass; a semi-pro travesty, a mock epic, a fiercely poetic mishmash, a terrible concoction of love and longing, hate, violence, death and monumental boredom that parodied itself and ended in victory.

"What the hell you doing with that fingernail polish?" I asked Ensign Ortman as I came down from watch in the radio shack aboard the *San Pablo* off the coast of Borneo.

"I'm treating these cards," he said.

Then I saw that Ortman was carefully painting both sides of each playing card with the little brush that came with each of the many bottles of fingernail polish he had standing on the bench in front of him.

"Why?" I asked.

"To preserve them."

"Christ, Ortman. They got more playing cards than food on this ship."

"I know," Ortman explained, "But I like this deck of cards."

As he finished painting each card he placed it neatly on top of the last until the whole deck was treated.

"It got a little thicker, didn't it?" I noted.

"What got thicker?" Ortman asked.

"The deck."

"Oh, I don't know," he said, picking up the deck and discovering that it was a solid block of stuck together cards. "Maybe a little thicker, not much though."

"Why don't you try dealing a hand, Ortman?" I asked, laughing.

"So they stuck together, that's all. What's so funny about that? Didn't I say I wanted to save this deck? Well, by Christ I embalmed it, didn't I?" And then Ortman laughed until he cried.

He was way, way up there, maybe thirty thousand feet or more, banking and rolling and putting on a show, and we were standing along the rail and craning up at him.

"Jesus, what a life," someone said. "Up there out of this crap—beautiful."

"And when he gets back, fresh eggs—carrier based, I bet," someone else said. "And a slug or two of whisky. They give those flyboys booze now, did you know that? Right on navy ships, what a deal."

"You mean to tell me you never had booze on a navy ship?" one of the gunners asked.

"I mean, booze served right at you, official booze," the other said.

"Official shit," the gunner said.

The fighter way up there was playing with the sky. He looked happy, stunting around with all that power and all that space under him. I'd always wanted to fly, maybe just to do what we thought he was doing up there, feeling free, no assignment, no mission, just flying for the hell of it.

"A Hellcat, isn't it?" the warrant officer said.

"Well it sure as hell ain't a Corsair," someone replied, and there was a phony snicker because no one ever mistook the gull wing of a Corsair for anything else.

Then the little speck that was a plane flashed into a cloud and made that sound that means it's on full rich in a power dive. In another flash it was out, and before it leveled at us someone yelled "Meatballs!" and we saw the red discs on the wings and fire at the gun ports. The stuff hit the water and then the steel bulkhead behind us and the Zero was gone.

Four of the men I'd eaten breakfast with were busted open against the bulkhead and splattered over the rest of us—just those four and not some other four or two or five, because the shells were spaced that way in the guns of that Zero, or because that hot pilot waggled a little or came a hair to port or starboard as he squeezed, or because the wind, or the air, or the yawing of the ship, or just because.

"It's chicken—the can's open. Here, for you," the voice said out of pitch blackness.

"Christ, Wharton," I answered. "Keep it yourself. If you found chicken around here you deserve it. You not hungry?"

"For Chrissake," Wharton said, his voice spaced between fire. "Here, goddammit, take it. If I hold it out much longer it'll be full of shrapnel and we'll both be screwed out of it."

I got out of the hole, but I couldn't straighten up and I stood there on the torn-up beach, bent double, about a yard high. It felt like it was all over. Up ahead I could see the medical pile beyond the dump and I made for it. It took forever. And when I got there there was just a tired-out corpsman.

"If you can just vomit," he said, and he gave me a cup of brine. "Here, throw it down." But I couldn't vomit and I let myself topple against the crates.

Then the doctor came. "Can't you straighten out?" he asked.

"So far, no," I said.

"Here," he said, sliding a sheet of plywood toward me, "I got to go over there," pointing to a black smoking fire across the sand and up into the first stand of trees. "You get down on this, on your back, and try to get yourself straight out."

In the hour he was gone, I worked against what felt like a powerfully incoming tide filled with knives cutting across my middle. And in the end, exhausted and afraid to move lest I snap back double again, I got myself flat.

"Just stay that way," the doctor instructed when he got back. "How long you been out here?"

"About a year, around here," I said.

"New Guinea before?"

"Yes."

He got down beside me and felt around. He asked, "How'd you like to go back to the States?"

"No jokes, doc," I said.

"No jokes," he replied.

I went double again when I got off the plywood and the doctor walked me that way down to the water, hailed an amphibious Jeep driven by a big black man, put a piece of paper—orders—in my hand, and I was taken off the beach. I came to alongside a radar pickett boat, and the marine hoisted me aboard as the Jeep banged against it. They put me on a pile of Mae Wests on the cabin deck and I fell asleep as the pickett boat turned to the open sea. How much later, I don't know, they woke me up and told me I should try to stand up and make it to the patrol craft bobbing alongside. It looked impossible even after I got up: first I'd be way above the deck of the PC, and then way below as the boats bobbed out of time. In the end I stepped off and someone caught me and I was asleep on canvas. Now and then I'd come to, and I could hear the diesel working hard in a choppy sea, the voices of men aboard and the sound of hand-sent code from the radio, someplace. I kept coming in and going out of the world and it felt like years were passing. Then they put me in a long wire basket and I was hoisted by cable to the high deck of a landing ship tank. The deck was piled high with crates of blood plasma, all around the 20 millimeter guns, and there was a red and white hand-painted sign on the bridge: THE HELPFUL. They took me down to the tank deck all fitted with triple-deck bunks—bunks for hundreds of men and all empty. A doctor came, took me to a lower bunk, told me to lie down, and began asking me questions as I fell asleep.

The doctor was there when I woke up. Everything seemed bright and noisy in a regular way.

"How you feel, Lieutenant?" the doctor asked with a big smile on his Irish-looking face.

I said, "Okay, I guess."

"How about a bowl of soup?" he asked.

The word "soup" sounded real and beautiful—as if I'd just learned the wonderful thing it stood for.

"That'd be fine," I said.

While he went to see about the soup, I pulled myself up and discovered that I could move much better. I felt like I'd been on a long and terrible drunk in which I wrestled and fought for days and had been beaten over and over. My insides felt like they'd come through my skin and that even though I could stand up straight and walk and bend, I'd have to be very careful not to break or tear anything.

"How long you think you slept?" the doctor asked when he brought the steaming soup.

"I don't know, but I feel a lot better."

"We helped you a little," he said, "but you went close to seventy-two hours. Do you know that we weighed you?"

"Weighed me? No, I don't remember that."

"I thought you didn't. That was something like twenty-four hours ago. What's your normal weight?"

"I used to go around a hundred and thirty-eight," I said.

"How much you think you weigh right now?"

"I don't know. I've lost, I know."

"Weismann," he said, "before you put that soup down, you just made a hundred and three."

"Doesn't surprise me," I said, "I've been wearing down, not enough sleep, blackouts, and then, poof!"

"It's an old story, Nothing to worry about. You'll be okay, just take it easy for a while; you can't win the war all by yourself."

That night *The Helpful* suddenly changed course and you could feel it being pushed at full ahead, high in the water and slapping under the bow. I asked a corpsman where we were headed and he said the word was that we were going to pick up survivors from the cruiser *Princeton* that was hit and burning. Hour after hour *The Helpful* kept pushing, and twice the guns rattled along her three hundred-foot deck—aircraft overhead. And then we slowed and finally stopped dead in the water.

Then they started coming down to the tank deck. Litter after litter bearing men burned black and crusty with their still liquid eyes peeking out, and parts gone from them. The smell of burned flesh, heavy, sickening but with a peculiar affinity for your own sense of smell, like the smell of your own sweat and your own blood and excrement, suddenly pervaded everything and every space. And they kept coming down with ears melted into their heads, noses gone, hands gone, and feet; arms and legs ending in pointed black sticks like the horsemen of Marino Marini. Then the saws and amputations, and I suddenly became the healthiest, strongest man in the world, helping hold, lifting, turning them over, lighting cigarettes and holding them into those holes in those faces of charcoal. I remember: what do you do with these cut-off hands and feet and arms and legs, as I handed another to a corpsman passing. Over the side to the sea, these parts of living men lost forever and the look of your own, so light in color, so beautiful, so strong and moist and good. And you felt ashamed. And how is it, I still ask and want no answer, that many of these men, crippled and burned, carried tremendous and painful erections. Oh body, we do not know you yet as we spend our time with "ram-jam radiation bulldozers, uncontaminated earth spreaders, / Troop-dropping trucks and mobile missile planters."

"But, doc," I said, "I really wanted to go back to my outfit; there's nothing back home for me now, not until this is all over and done. I've got hundreds of friends all over thousands of square miles out here, but it just didn't work. There I am, doc, on that peaceful beach the other side of Henderson Field, just waiting for orders; plenty of ice cold beer, nurses even, and a great place to swim. So I come out all tan and feeling great and stretch out in one of those honest-to-God canvas deck chairs to read that last book by Oscar Levant and really everything is just great, fine, couldn't maybe be better. And I'm feeling so lucky and so grateful that I can't wait to get back and do what I can, when, Jesus, I'm doubled up again and I hear rockets that aren't there and see faces I thought I'd forgotten. Doc, what the hell is this?"

Lt. Commander Hollis Winter, M.D. said, "Look, Weismann, it's easy. Let's say you're a woman, the story works better that way, okay? Well, you're a woman about twenty-eight, say, and you have a son age three, okay? And you were told when you had that baby that you couldn't have another. So you got this three-year-old boy, and you know it's the only one of your own you can ever have. So you come out on the porch. It's springtime and everything is just about perfect. Then, as you look out across the porch railing, you see a Mack truck coming fast down the street and in a flash you see your baby boy smashed all over that truck.

Now I ask you, Weismann, how do you think you'd feel if you were that woman?"

"Christ, doc, you know how I'd feel."

"Okay. Now let's repeat this same event, this same smashing to death of your only, never-to-be-had-again son every day for a couple of years, and have you see it as if for the first time, every time. How do you think you'd feel after a couple of years of that?"

"It'd kill me."

"Weismann," Dr. Winter said, "that's about where you're at, only you're not going out on that porch any more; you're going home."

Stanza fifty-five has the man with the word leave the military behind him, while the object of a boyhood dream of mine—a really flyable ornithopter—is made the questionable property of a Puerto Rican advertising outfit and used to tow a sure sign that the word was not heard.

He left Camp Pinkerton while the shadows were still underfoot, and overhead
An ornithopter owned by a Puerto Rican ad agency, trailed a fretwork sign
That read emit now RUO NI EVOL SI YTIRUCES LAICOS from the north,
And from the south: SOCIAL SECURITY IS LOVE IN OUR OWN TIME.

She was standing outside the dime store in Gary, Indiana and I was coming up from the South. "My name's Jeff," she said. "Just call me Jeff."
She was in sagging black and tired, but she was beautiful too, and I went with her. The room was cool and as I stood there I realized how worn out I was. Framed over the dresser was a photograph of a young woman standing on a carved wooden porch with her arms around a man who looked like Douglas Fairbanks.
"Far from Gary," Jeff said, "and long ago." She pulled down the buff colored shade and the room turned into a late Rembrandt. "He's gone," she continued. "Killed at the mills. Never shoulda left Valparaiso . . . you're tired, why don't you lay down?"
I was asleep before the question died in the air, and a dream was rolling out—a dream of the night sky of Gary from the first time I'd watched it boiling black and orange-vermilion above the blast furnaces

and stacks when I was twelve. And under the sky the Douglas Fairbanks man was calling, "My God! My God!" but it was too late: he was dead in a photograph with a coming-apart oak frame over the dresser and the molten steel swallowed him up and burned him away, long ago.

When I put my hat back on I tried to say something, but nothing came. "It's all right, all okay," Jeff said. "I was bushed too, and I never woulda come back to rest if you didn't come along."

I used to see them in the morning when I got back from the midnight-to-eight at the coliseum. They'd be waiting for their taxis under striped canopies outside apartment buildings with names like "Terrace" and "Crest" and "Arms" lettered in gold across the fanlights. Beautifully dressed, they were in fitted suits, silk stockings with seams running perfectly up the calves from unscuffed high-heeled slippers; and their faces and throats were clear and white and held with the consciousness of models who know how delicate and transient their eligibility is. *Executive, Personal* and *Very Private Secretaries,* they were, who'd moved up to Chicago's 1942 Gold Coast where the hotel-sweet big bands played in "The Pump Room" and the microphone was set just right so you could hear the hushed dreamy laughter in the background, and every now and then the clink of a glass when you turned it up on your Atwater-Kent or Crosley, no matter where you were.

I lived on the Gold Coast—in a back apartment with wooden steps down four floors to an alley where bent men ate Gold Coast garbage out of Gold Coast garbage cans in the snow—all the time I taught those radiomen-gunners for the United States Army Air Force, and it didn't feel all that different from Gary. But I knew it was, with the likes of Jeff and her Fairbanks man losing out on that land bought by the United States Steel Corporation thirty-seven years before, and the likes of the means and protection that percolated all the way down to those executive, personal and very private women going to cover-up work at nine. Of course it was all that different, no matter how it seemed; and it was that difference, that spread, I wanted to make in the opening of stanza fifty-six:

That night, between the tarnished gold coast and the flaming skies of Gary,
He watched the thousands go in guilt-edged boredom,
Curiosity, ignorance and emptiness
Down the streets and through the concrete holes
Into Chicago's Soldier Field,
To see and hear Young Billy Migraine,
The crusading self-evaginist, go vertigo and hypnotize
Half a hundred thousand with himself on snowbird snuff,
About a no-down-payment Jesus who consecretes the status quo.

And from that spread of differences come all those who are the same in their boredom, curiosity, ignorance and emptiness. "I come; I come," they cadence across the grass memorial to buried Christian soldiers.

"Lead Thou me on," they sing to the pitch talk of the everted pusher, no matter his name: the young Reverend Billy Jack with eyes seeing straight through the fire and brimstone to the quiff he'll take a little later in the shadow of the tent outside Ripley, Ohio; the Prophet Bob Williams Junior with the photoengraving of himself in jockey shorts lifting weights on the *Love Offering* envelope, outside Sheboygan, Wisconsin, or the Reverend Billy Migraine, Anywhere, U.S.A.

The "Holy Rollers" used to meet in a place on National Avenue near Ninth in Milwaukee, back in 1929. Before the Holy Rollers took it over it had been a grocery store that never appeared to be doing any business. I used to sit on the concrete steps in front of Loretta Gergo's father's saloon talking to Loretta while the place was still a grocery store with two bare electric light bulbs shining out the two windows across the street. I used to look across at those bulbs a lot when I was sitting so close to Loretta I could feel her heart beat. I used to talk to her and put my arms around her, and all the time I'd keep staring at those lights across the street. It was easier that way: not seeing, just feeling how Loretta was taking to my lies about where I'd been and what I'd done, and what I was going to do the next day and the next year and for all my life. And then one night when I looked over there the lights were gone and the store had moved out. Two men came one day and painted the bottom halves of the show windows solid black, and soon after that Loretta and I used to sit in front of her father's saloon and listen to the shouting and singing of the Holy Rollers.

And pretty soon I was standing at the front door looking in, and then sitting in the empty back row listening to their preacher talk about the strength of Jesus when Jesus possessed a truly repentant sinner. The preacher was a tall, skinny man who usually wore overalls and sounded like he was from some place like Arkansas. Every time I heard him preach he got everybody stirred up, and then, one by one, the people would come up to the front to testify. And even when there were only a few people in the place, he still got them to call out and yell as if they were a hundred. They often brought rolled-up newspapers with them, and after the preacher had gotten their spirits up, and while the testimonials were being shouted out about how Jesus came into their lives, right into their bodies and intoxicated them with joy, they'd begin swatting each other with those rolled-up newspapers. The longer and louder the testimonial, the harder they swatted each other and the louder they all got.

I took a rolled-up *Milwaukee Journal* with me one Saturday night and sat in the empty back as usual. After they got to swatting each other, a very small woman with a bald spot whacked me on my shoulder and I whacked her back. This must have been taken as a sign of my coming into the Holy Rollers because most of the men and women in the place that night came around and swatted me all over. For a while after that I used to come in the evening with my newspaper (once with the whole Sunday edition, Rotogravure Section and all) and wait for the swatting to begin. It was fun and everybody appeared to enjoy it even though they didn't laugh, and very seldom smiled. I got to the point where I'd prepared a testimonial, based for the most part on Jack London's short story, "To Build a Fire"—that one about the man in the frozen north with just a few matches, maybe only one, trying to build a fire; and when he does just get it going, it melts the snow from a bough of the tree under which he'd foolishly built his fire and the snow slides down and extinguishes it. There was something in it, too, as I remember, about how the man was thinking of cutting open his faithful dog and putting his freezing hands inside to thaw them. But I never gave my testimonial, I just thought about it an awful lot. Instead, it seems, I went to the Holy Rollers' Convention in Waukesha, about twenty-five miles west of Milwaukee. And there in a park-like place on the edge of town five hundred or a thousand gathered to hear a whole slew of men and women shout the intoxication and jump and kick and roll, some wildly together, in the grass.

I never made much of the Holy Rollers. I never connected what they were doing with the vague concept I had of religion. To me, the mood and actions that went with their meetings in Milwaukee and with the day I spent among them in Waukesha at age fourteen, was more like those I'd known at the circus, or at a friendly fight at the skating rink over on

Greenbush Street, or like what often happened after a Boys' Tech-Washington High School football game. And even though the men and women who preached appeared dead serious, I still thought of them in the way I thought of the three-legged man I'd seen with Ringling Brothers and Barnum and Bailey: the freak show guide stopped in front of the three-legged man's place, introduced him and told something about where he'd been born, that both his parents had only two legs each, something about his family life and growing up, and about the tailor who makes his three-legged pants, and such; and then the three-legged man produced a football, put it down on the ground, and with his right and left feet firmly planted, kicked the ball with his middle foot. And then as the group began to move on to the six-hundred pound "Fattest Woman in the World" in the next enclosure, the three-legged man went into his own pitch to sell photographs of himself in a swimming suit. With both the Holy Rollers and the three-legged man, I felt a mixture of the macabre, the sad, and the funny. With them, I never felt anything like the presence of strange power and people caught up in a terror generated by a leader as I did when I heard the evangelist Bob Williams Junior in a tent outside Sheboygan, Wisconsin in 1935.

It wasn't even a big tent; maybe it had folding chairs and benches for three or four hundred people. But when husky young Bob Williams Junior came on the platform after the guitar music in his tight-fitting black pants and white silk blouse open at the throat and began to talk slowly in a strong low voice about evil and its agent the devil, and how not even a baby is immune to evil's disease, the vilest, most deadly of all—when he held various statue-like poses as the reed organ backed him up, I could feel what he was doing with those people—as if they were all just one frail shell-shocked kid. And at just the right moment, and perhaps by using confederates, when some people were already crying out loud, he pointed out into the audience and called for this person and that person to come forward in a public sign of repentance and an invitation for Jesus to come into their hearts and be "loved, loved, loved; oh sweet love!" And as the women and girls came up, husky young Bob Williams

Junior put his arms around them and they moaned and cried all over his silk blouse. And then even men and boys came up, all the while the reed organ, played by a plump older woman who looked very much like Bob Williams Junior, and hooked up to a public address system, played a kind of waltz-march and young male and female assistants passed out *Love Offering* envelopes with Bob's picture in jockey shorts on the front and a place to write your own name for Jesus.

Young Bob Williams Junior had a lot of the same thing working for him that that man of fifty years had working for him on the edge of the Wisconsin State Fair grounds in 1931. He had a huge black Packard sedan parked on the grass with the back end jutting out toward one of the side paths to the midway. Folded out from the back of the Packard there was a platform like a very oversize trunk rack, and behind that an eight-foot backdrop of black velvet. This fifty-year-old man who looked very much like Jack Holt with a little of Adolf Menjou mixed in, stood on the platform with the black velvet behind him and talked about good health. He said he would soon be seventy years old, but that most people took him for forty-five or fifty and that he himself felt like he was eighteen or twenty, and, in fact, performed *in all ways* as if he actually was that young.

For a long time he talked as if his mission in life was only to tell people how precious good health is, and how important sleep and exercise are. Gradually, and as the crowd got bigger, he worked his theme around to food and the digestive system. From the top edge of the velvet backdrop he pulled down highly colored charts showing the insides of the human body, especially intestines. The last of a series of charts he showed was the biggest and most highly colored. With his pure white baton, he pointed to the chart and said, "Of course you recognize this as the human intestinal tract, the source of most of your pain and discomfort and unhappiness, whether you think it's in your brain, your heart, liver, lungs, sexual organs or appendages. But do you know *whose* intestinal tract this is? Do you know the name of the man whose body this is part of? And do you know that this man, who was loved and admired by everyone in this audience over twelve or fourteen years of age, died at the early age *of thirty-one years?* These, ladies and gentlemen," he said, "are the intestines of Rodolpho d'Antonguolla, the great movie star who all of you knew as just Rudolph Valentino —dead now, at the age of thirty-one, these past five years. Here are the intestines that, as long as they were treated right, thrilled us all in *The Four Horsemen of the Apocalypse, The Sheik, Blood and Sand, The Eagle* and many more. But ladies and gentlemen," he said in a more confidential and professional tone, "Rudolph Valentino didn't treat his intestines right. Now, what did Rudolph Valentino do that many of you do, many of you who don't feel as fit and vigorous in *all ways,* I mean, yes, *in all ways* as fit and vigorous as you deserve to feel? Here," he said, pulling down another chart, "are the intestines of Rudolph Valentino in the morning—let's say on a Monday morning.

"All right, he gets up and eats breakfast, a good healthy breakfast and it comes down here," pointing with his baton, "down here into the lower intestinal tract, and because he's too busy *or because he doesn't* care, Rudolph Valentino let that breakfast food pack in *and remain* there right where you see it here in red. All right," he continued, pulling down another chart, "what did Rudolph Valentino do next? Well, he ate lunch, and here it is, in red, packed right down on top of his breakfast now showing in green, because, ladies and gentlemen, if Rudolph Valentino doesn't get rid of that breakfast pretty soon it will, in fact, be green. All right, let's see what we have on this next medical chart. It's dinnertime and Rudolph Valentino has had his dinner, a good big rich dinner. And here it is in red, packed down on top of the green mass of his breakfast and lunch and a sandwich he ate between shooting scenes, perhaps for *The Sheik* or *Blood and Sand.* All right, now night comes and what does Rudolph Valentino do? Does he have a bowel movement? No. Does he see to it to help nature so he can eliminate that hardening green mass? No. Does he get rid of it? No. You know what Rudolph Valentino did? That great movie star took it to bed with him! Yes, that's what he did, took it to bed with him. And day after day he built up this green, and night after night he took it to his Hollywood bed with him until his whole system was clogged up, and, ladies and gentlemen . . . he died; died of simple ancient constipation: C-O-N-S-T-I-P-A-T-I-O-N."

At that spelling out, two girls, about nineteen or twenty, in black silk stockings, high-heeled pumps and tutus came out of the Packard sedan with baskets full of bottles of pink liquid and pictures of the "Woman in Black" at Rudolph Valentino's grave. The bottles cost a dollar each, three for two-fifty—a high price for 1931—and an awful lot were bought. The pitchman then got down from the platform, went around to the front seat of the Packard, had a drink from a pint bottle of whisky, lit a cigarette and walked around on the grass for a few minutes. And then he started the spiel all over again.

I hung around listening and watching this man for more than two hours and figured that if each bottle and its contents cost him twenty cents, and he was averaging about ninety cents on each one, then he was making a profit of about eighteen dollars every time he made a complete pitch. Even when I considered his rest periods, he was making three pitches and over fifty dollars an hour. I remember thinking that with the Fair open about fifteen hours each day, he could certainly work for twelve, and that meant he could come through with about six hundred dollars over and above the cost of the de-constipating fluid he was selling. Even with his overhead, I figured he was clearing around five hundred dollars a day as he moved from state fair to state fair to county fair to circus and carnival. I remember he had Florida plates on the Packard and an immense diamond (but maybe it was only a zircon) on his finger.

And I remember thinking of how, maybe, he could have been selling something he called Jesus or redemption just as successfully as he sold his pink purgative, like Elmer Gantry, maybe. But the feeling I had about the fifty-year-old constipation man was very different from how I felt about husky young Bob Williams Junior. The fifty-year-old man, preaching on a text of Rudolph Valentino's intestines, was highly entertaining and ridiculously funny to me. Young Bob Williams Junior dealt in something else "To prove his light in mob psychology darkness . . . To the music of electric guitars," and whatever travesty it was it succeeded in exploiting and tragically damaging trust, no matter how ignorantly or mistakenly placed, and in shifting focus from the personal malaise and the incompleteness of people to a grotesquely debased and ludicrous image of a

forgiving savior—himself, young Bob Williams Junior—or my own Billy
Migraine and all their likes.

So, in my poem I have my man with the word thunder it out, then
shriek it into a slice of silence in Chicago's Soldier Field while another,
latter day Bob Williams Junior with all of Barnum, electronics, the
media, management, politics and advance billing behind him, gives
promises of free piggy-back rides on a motorized plastic Jesus while he
becomes a millionaire over and over.

Thinking of great numbers and the scatter of probability for almost
    anything,
The man with the word filed in with the mob to a seat on the fifty-
    yard line.
High on the rim of the Field, under the moonless sky by the lake,
He watched Young Billy career in his checkered coat and movie face,
Right down to the semi-final when he called
For a hundred thousand safety matches to be lit
To prove his light in mob psychology darkness.
And while the matches burned in something like noiselessness,
The man with the word thundered it out, then shrieked it staccato;
But not a match died out, nor was a voice borne high or low
Until Young Billy Migraine called for personally autographing Jesus
To the music of electric guitars.

Little wonder then that over Chicago's Soldier Field:

The sky threw up, and the man with the word
Went by a side gate to the open road
Past places that still await their names,
To Billings on the Yellowstone.

My calling up the name of Billings, Montana was not just a matter
of chance, nor was it merely the ding-dong ring of the names that had
me refer to that town as "Billings on the Yellowstone," though chance
and music are always pretty much in everything. I drove slowly through
Billings late one July night in 1938, found it blacked-out and shut down,
so I drove on out to the edge, pulled into an open field and went to sleep.
When I woke up and got out to walk the kinks out of my back and legs,
I saw that a carnival was setting up a little further in toward town. After
breakfast in a little café where the conversation stopped as I came in, I
went out looking for those prehistoric remains that had been discovered
in some caves the year before. I never found them, but by then the sun
was warm and I stretched out in the grass near the river and slept for a
couple of hours.

By noon the carnival was just about up—a Ferris wheel, a merry-go-
round, a crack-the-whip, a fortune teller, a big bingo set-up, a pellet-gun
range and lots of games of chance. I bought an ice cream sandwich from
a man stocking the cold box in a little blue and white striped stand with
the name, NORTH POLE, painted on a post that stuck out the top.

"You looking for work?" the ice cream man asked.

"Not particularly," I said.

"What do you mean by that?"

"Nothing," I said. "Just that I'm not looking very hard, that's all."

"Ever run a numbers wheel?"

"No, not much. What kind?"

"The kind that's worth running and that'll guarantee you a quarter of the take," he smiled.

"Me, or the guy who owns it?"

"You," he said. "The guy who handles the wheel. The owner gets his, don't worry."

"They always do." I asked, "Who owns it?"

"I do," he answered. "Come on over and have a look."

I went over with him to a stand that had a sign, WIN BIG ON THE BIG WHEEL, painted across the front. The big wheel was mounted on a four-by-four at one end of the stand. It was a handsome object with ten carved spokes, a large center area and a wide outer edge that carried the widely spaced numbers, one to twenty-five. It was painted in red, white, black, blue and gold and looked like something off a nineteenth-century carousel or Sicilian cart. Very closely spaced brass-headed nails, hundreds of them it appeared, stood out from lines that radiated from the center. Of the hundreds of spaces between these lines, only twenty-five carried numbers; the rest were blanks—no-wins. A springy piece of metal extended down from above the wheel to a level below the shafts of the nails, so that when the wheel was spun it made a loud clacking sound. When the wheel stopped the metal came to rest between two nails and pointed either to a number or to a blank.

"Not such hot odds," I noted. "Out of all that, there's only twenty-five of those little spaces that got any numbers at all, and then you've got to hit your special number to win."

"We go as high as twenty-to-one odds if we got a good player going," the man reasoned. "We'll pay twenty bucks for every single he shows. They put their chips down on the numbers here on the counter; we can't use money so they buy chips—white, ten cents; blue, twenty-five; red, fifty; and gold, a dollar—any amount on any number, and then you spin the wheel. Every time they lose, you win."

"Why the kewpie dolls?" I asked, looking at two shelves of them behind the wheel.

"Sometimes you can make it easier if the guy loses a lot—just give him a doll for being a good sport, you know. You pay for the dolls you give away, fifty cents apiece."

"It's okay," I concluded. "But it's not for me."

"You run one before, right?"

"I've seen them before."

"Well," the man said, "if you're wondering if there's a brake, the answer is yes—works against the axle."

"No," I said, "I wasn't wondering about that, I just don't like to stand up all day and keep talking."

"I need a man on the Ferris wheel tonight," the man countered. "You can sit down all the time it's going."

I ran the Ferris wheel that night outside Billings on the Yellowstone. Around eleven a fight broke out under the sign, WIN BIG ON THE BIG WHEEL, and in a matter of minutes the whole stand was torn down and people were running away with the kewpie dolls. There were Indians in the crowd and one of them was still fighting with the operator, the ice cream man, when the police came on. When they drove off they had two Indians in the back of the patrol car. In the poem I call them a Blackfoot and a Kootenai, and they ride where I have my man with the word ride— to be dumped off "hard in a gray ghost town."

Along the river where the outcropping prehistoric remains,
A Memphis gambling outfit was working hard in its carnival guise
To get to Great Falls in the clear.
The snag-numbered wheels and skin games with five-sided bones
Were slicing the deficit when a Blackfoot and a Kootenai, too
    suddenly fleeced,
Lashed the debonair concessionaire to the other side of his birthday

With smartly matched lacings from straps of plaited thong and
   horsehair.
The man with the word had witnessed it all,
So the Billings police took him off to one side
To get his statement of what had happened before and after the
   brawl.
Tell us, they said, in your very own words, how it went pell-mell to
   melee;
And the man said he needed only one to tell, and that one was jelly.
The Sergeant said he'd better be careful, sir,
About withholding an officer and resisting evidence,
But the man kept answering with jelly, loud and clear,
Until the Sergeant took his fingerprints and turned him over to the
   State Patrol.
In their souped-up Mercury with automatic guns in the upholstery
   they told him,
By damn, he sounded like one of those liberals from Eastern
   Montana State Normal,
So forthwith they sped him into the Bitterroot Range
And dumped him hard in a gray ghost town.

Maybe any sort of event, any kind of action could have gotten my
man with the word from Soldier Field Chicago to Billings on the
Yellowstone to the headwaters of the Missouri River—or he needn't have
gone that way at all. But some place along the line I felt an asking to
bring my man to where a pure chance kind of gambling was going on. In
my experience there's something very special hangs in the air around
games of chance played for real stakes. People I've known for a long time
seem to turn into other unknown people, to become something else, take
on other characters and show faces I'd never seen before the wheel is spun
or the dice are rolled out with a good chunk of their money riding with
them. The most reasonable, down to earth, two-times-two-equals-four
people suddenly expect the answer to be five or three or even eleven.
They believe the dice can hear, that they have feelings and can be offend-

ed by bad talk and coddled into cooperation by good. They feel hot or cold, ready to come out on track seven or lie dead in the shed, right or wrong by what amounts to commands from the way the dice fall, from a spirit that enters the room or gets spontaneously generated in the air around the wheel or the crap table.

I'm not talking about the guy who stops by for a couple of rolls, to try a pass or two on his way home with the change or few bucks in his side pants pocket. I'm talking about the guy who troubles to find out when and where a game is coming up, who waits for it to open, who keeps his money in three or four places in his clothing as an easy mechanical check of how deep in he's going—and he's usually got most of the green folded in his last stash, the bundle that'll bring him back up if he really goes under. I'm talking about guys like Hawk Hydal, my roommate in Sheboygan in 1935—the kind of man who believes he can *see* that the last digit on the next-to-appear Chevrolet license plate will be a six, nothing else, just a six, and who believes that *he,* not fate or destiny or God, screwed him up when the Chevrolet turns into the drag with the number five where the six should be.

There's a very rare, super-refined air around where chance rules and people believe they know how it will unfold. In such air it feels like anything you want to have happen can happen; and if you do your part just right, then, by God, it *will* rain, smack out of a cloudless sky. So, maybe if *The Word,* the question of questions, the answer of answers, the most of all the best, the Alpha and the Omega, was to be voiced in the hope that for the very first time it would be heard, then one place it should be called out is over the spinning wheel and the rolling dice. In Billings on the Yellowstone chance is tampered with, the wheel is fixed, the game is crooked, ("snag-numbered wheels and skin games with five-sided bones"), and my man with the word never calls it out. He just says it over and over to some policemen, like he was taking the Fifth Amendment, over and over until they dump him off in a Montana ghost town.

From the lumber of the forsaken town he makes a raft and launches it toward the spot where the fur traders used to come down the Missouri to the Mississippi to Pierre Laclede's old post where St. Louis now stands:

On a raft of shingles, clapboards and saloon doors,
He floated away from Three Forks, down the Missouri,
Across the plains of North and South Dakota,
Nebraska, Kansas, Iowa and Missouri, calling jelly all the way
Along the river and into Bismark, Pierre, the City of the Sioux,
Council Bluffs, Omaha, Atchison, Leavenworth and Kansas City, clear
To the Father of Waters, seventeen miles above Saint Louis.

From the first time I could hear my father talk, and feel I knew what he was saying—long before I went to school—I got a picture of a man with lots of friends who still wandered alone or almost alone in the world. For longer than it perhaps should have been, the world to me was America, the United States of America, from "Fifty-four-forty or fight" to the Rio Grande, and "from the rockbound coast of Maine to the sunny shores of California." I read Frederick Jackson Turner's *The Frontier in American History* while I was still in grade school. I read Walter Prescott Webb's *The Great Plains* the year it came out, and thirty years after that I got to know the man, eat over an open fire with him and—with Roy Bedicheck, Harry Ransom, Frank Wardlaw and J. Frank Dobie—drink Jack Daniels with him. From the first pictures of the world that my father drew in me, the clearest and most powerful ones were of the West. They were big pictures of immense lands, rivers, deserts, gorges and mountains all against the kind of sky I saw when I lay in a backyard in Milwaukee and stared straight up. And they were pictures that didn't fade; pictures that got made into drawings and paintings long before I'd seen the places from where my father's voice had brought them. And then when I'd gotten there and walked where my father had walked, the places asked to hear my own voice if only in lots and lots of soliloquies never completed over the years:

In September the sun goes early down the edge of Wyoming;
Half-past six and the twilight dark is coming, as he came
To the long abandoned jail open wide to the empty slanting
    countryside
Around the forgotten remains of a nameless town.
No one was there, nor was there any reason to be,
Unless to escape the night beside the road,
Shielded some from the wind
Turning, now, to cold.

With a split erratic lying near the stoop, he propped up the three-
    legged bed,
Spread a double sheet from the *Deadwood Times* across the tired
    springs,
Ate a biscuit from his bindle in the dark,
Buttoned up and went down deep into Wyoming sleep.

The night raced past, dreamless, fast,
No different from thousands he'd lost before,
Until his eyes dawned up toward the zenith and gleamed a way
Between the jailhouse rafters clear through the colorless and blue,
Into the light-year energy out of that Wyoming place and hour
To the time that's absolute and the space that's only time.

"And now," my father said, after covering the whole floor of Ed Strachota's saloon with suds from the mop, "before we dry it up for the boss, I'll draw you a picture of the saddest, most God-forsaken state in the union." And then with the handle end of the mop he scored through the yellow-white Fels Naptha foam to the dark wet oak below, one single straight line all the way from the State Street plate glass window to the Family Entrance at the other end.

"What state is it, Pa?" I asked in the early morning of that day in 1923.

"It's South Dakota," he answered. "Too far one way to be Wyoming, and too far another way to be Texas or New Mexico." And then my father sudsed the floor again and drew the West beyond and south of South Dakota, and I saw him walking in it, young, on the go to the sea; and I heard him playing in the wind, his own shiny Honer Marine Band harmonica, and dying away.

In 1960, on stationery of the Rice Hotel in Houston, Walter Prescott Webb sent me the promised foreword to a little book I'd written thirteen years before. "Change it any way you want, Weismann," he wrote. "But this is pretty much what I can do about it now." At the end, the foreword says that, "This pioneer story is told so often because it is always new. And it is always new because what happened in that period can never happen again. There is but one pioneer period in a nation's history. It is the period of youth, of adventure, of great expectations; and we will cherish the memory of it forever."

In 1944 the eastbound hospital train stopped on an open track outside North Platte, Nebraska and stood waiting for the regular one going west to the war. The ambulatories got off and stood there on the flatland and stared up and out along the silence. A railroad checker came down the line checking the truck journals, seeing if any hotboxes were developing. As he dropped the lid of each journal housing, he let it drop against his hand and then eased his hand out so that you couldn't hear the cover come to rest.

"Why that way?" a flyer who'd been hit over Saigon, French Indochina asked.

"Orders," the checker said. "Hospital train: no noise." Then from a growing speck in the east, out toward Buffalo Bill's old home that he'd called "Scout's Rest Ranch," the sound of the westbound grew closer, measuring that long straight line my father had drawn for a state just to the north.

The sleet kept piling up on the windshield. The wipers had given up and now my hands were too cold to heat the glass from inside. I drove looking out the side window of the Model-A Ford I'd bought from the Milwaukee Park Commission in 1945. It was close to ten, about five miles outside Atchison, Kansas, and I pulled into the first lights that flashed "GAS—EATS."

I was eating my hamburger standing by a barrel-shaped stove when two men in black suits, black overcoats, black gloves and hats came in. They ordered fried egg sandwiches and brought them up to the stove where I nursed my coffee.

"A bitch out there tonight," I said.

"Been a bitch all day," the taller one said. "That Model-A out there yours?"

"It's mine," I confirmed. "Can't see out to drive."

"Get him to give you a potato," the shorter one suggested.

"A potato?" I asked.

"He's got potatoes here," he said. "Just cut it in half and rub it on your windshield—or a onion, it'll keep it from icing up."

"Really, will it?"

"That's what we're doing," the tall one said.

"I'll be damned." I inquired, "What you driving?"

"Cadillac," the tall one said. "Cadillac hearse."

"Funeral?"

"Not yet," the tall one explained. "But when it is, it'll be a shut coffin deal; you should see him."

"Bad, huh?"

"Here's this drunk," the tall man said, "smoking in bed back there—musta been smoking, how else, and drunk—and lights the bed on fire and don't even know it. The whole goddamn room went up, burned through the floor, and he drops down to the next and burns a hole right through that one, and down he goes into the basement, what's left of him. We come out there to pick up the body and you can't tell what it is—a pig or a burned-up side of beef or a pile of wool melted in a ball— just a stinkin' black lump. You should see it."

"Where you got to take it?" I asked.

"Christ, to Hell and gone—two hundred fuckin' miles west of here, to his wife," the short man said, "in a goddamn no-man's land."

He was hoeing a field of corn across the road west of Kahoka, Missouri and I was absently feeding the last of my Mexican *Entero Vioformo* pills to some chickens as I waited for a ride in 1936. After the chickens wandered off and I stood there wondering what kind of eggs they'd maybe never lay again, I called out across the road, "Awful hot, eh?"

"Terrible hot," the man called back, straightening up and pressing his hands into the small of his back.

"Keeps on, it'll burn up your corn."

The man answered, "Maybe. You don't farm, do you?"

"No."

"Takes some faith," the man explained. "You know what the Lord said: wherever I am, there also shall my servant be."

"The West is where I should've been born," my father once told me, and he was talking about himself. "And it should've been a long time ago," he said, "then you would've been born there too, if I'd got married; but then maybe I wouldn't have married your mother unless she'd been out there too. But long ago would've been the best time, when the trains were there, but before everybody got the idea to ride them."

And I remember later when Ed Wolfe, my father's old friend from grade school days, came back from Germany and my father was gone, someplace.

"How long you been living in this dump, Stella?" he asked my mother. "And where the hell's the furniture?"

"He's been gone a long time, Ed," my mother told him, "almost a year."

"What've you been living on?"

"A little from here and a little from there," she explained. "We get along."

"But the furniture," Ed Wolfe said. "You used to have a lot of furniture—where'd it go?"

"It never was much, Ed. We're both sitting on chairs, aren't we? It just got awful cold last winter, Ed. We burned it up."

"How've you been eating, Stella?" he asked.

"You saw the kids, Ed—how'd they look to you?"

"Fine, just fine, Stella," he said. "But he sends you money, doesn't he?"

"Fifty dollars last Christmas, And something on the kids' birthdays."

"Where is he, Stella?"

"The last letter, about two months ago, was stamped Beatty, Nevada."

"Jesus Christ!" Ed Wolfe exclaimed. "Beatty—why, Fritz and me were out there the year the earthquake hit Frisco—we were calling ourselves house painters then—Christ, I'll never forget, never—we were rolling up getting set to go on to California when some guy starts on a mouth organ, and Fritz says, he says to me, 'Ed, it's okay, hunky-dory with me: you go ahead, Ed. Go on out to that San Fernando Valley, but I'm going to hop the next one going east no matter how far I got to walk.' I bet he was thinking about you, Stella, way back there—fact is that's what he said. 'You can go on out to that San Fernando Valley if that's what you want, but I'm going back.' That's what he said, Stella, honest to God. Fritz makes mistakes sometimes, but he never forgets—he's got a heart of gold, so help me, Stella, pure gold."

Stanza sixty-one of the poem has my man with the word beach his raft where the waters of the Missouri and the Mississippi meet. And like every one of those letters we ever corked into a bottle and threw into a river, lake or sea, like every one of those notes we scrawled on the undersides of bridges, on walls, fences, boxcars, rusting boilers, chimneys, water tanks, boats and bombs, he letters out the word on his used-up raft and walks into St. Louis.

> He beached his raft where the waters meet and watched them prove
>   they were one.
> With a brush of river rushes and paint of the brightest clay,
> He lettered out the word as a sign on the darkened raft
> And stood it against an oak growing gray in the waters' Y.
> He walked the tufted banks below the bluffs, the sands
> Along the coming peneplain, past the bridges spanning east,
> South out of the west to Looey's name-sainted City of the Blues.

All my life I've been a sucker for the darkened dive where someone is playing a piano. I've got my special tastes for what I like best to hear, but for me, they're just broad enough. And I usually gravitate to where no one in the place appears to be hearing the piano until it stops. I never went much for those places where some good-enough piano player is set up with an oversize grand and the customers, usually in couples, sit on upholstered stools right up against the lid and use it for a bar and ask for "old favorites." And I guess I don't care much for the piano player who talks more than he plays—about the number he's about to play, how it was when he played in "Frisco," "L.A." or at the such-and-such groovy club in New York, or how everything fits into some usually outrageous fantasy of the history of the blues, barrel house or subcultures. I care for the piano player who, no matter how far gone he is, feels to me that he isn't a whole man—no matter how small or big—until he sits down, looks at the keys as if he'd never seen them before, but guesses that they can open all the doors, and then goes ahead and opens them and goes on through, and keeps on going through.

Years ago, maybe I was eighteen, there was a woman that played in an Italian bar on Jefferson Street in Milwaukee's Third Ward. She was that kind of piano player. I used to be able to pretty well describe the hole in my spirit that her playing could fill. I'd be sitting someplace, or work-ing, or listening to somebody saying something at me, or listening to myself saying something at somebody else in the morning, in the after-noon or in the middle of the night, and I'd feel that aching hole. Sometimes I could beat it across town to Jefferson Street, if the time was right and she was there, and slow down half a block away and then saunter through that door as if I didn't give a damn for all the time I didn't have, as if I were Mr. Complete just stopping for a beer that I could take or leave, no matter, and as if I wouldn't hear the piano if it was stuffed, playing right into my ears. I'd come in and stand near the door, up where it said JEFFERSON INN in red, white and green in an arch across the window, look at the gilded pictures on the open cigar box covers and read the labels on the bottles and the marks on the bar—while that woman to whom I never said a word, just went on filling that hole in me with such great gifts that they sometimes made the rest of me feel that it would have to find a way to improve.

There was a man in St. Louis, a black man, who played in a bar on Sarah Street when I was getting ready to teach those radiomen-gunners. Even though he was propped up on a little platform right back of the far end of the bar with all those people and noise, he played as if he was a lone survivor on a raft becalmed in the open sea. I used to walk over to Sarah Street after my night class in communications math, after I'd sat through a couple of hours of being reminded of still one more gap in my education, and stand there listening to that man who seemed to be playing out his whole damnation and redemption. I'd stare straight down into my glass that would open up—the longer that man played—to more of the star-marked infinity than ever eluded the still-lifes of Claez or Renoir. And as that "half-gone son of the Proclamation" played on, the spirit got mended, filled, made whole again as the vessel itself got rocked "through the doors of the lock" and launched into the wide open sea again.

My "half-gone son of the Proclamation" of stanza sixty-two is that black man in a rundown bar on Sarah Street, St. Louis in 1942.

> He turned with the town away from the river and the cast iron-gated fronts
> Into streets the flatboatmen and sidewheel trade helped
> To plank and cobble below the tar and cement.
> A piano was being played by a half-gone son of the Proclamation
> Stilted up on a dunnage stand behind the handwrought bar,

Under the neon lights jumping in a jack-knife dive on Rummage
   Street.
The melody was anchored in rhythmic pitch that kept the flukes
   from rusting,
And by the chain he rocked the vessel through the doors of the lock
Between the high morning river and the low down twilight blue.

Here, into this, the word ought to be called out with real hopes for
its being heard. But maybe the music was already too close to being what
the word was meant only to recall. So I have my man with the word begin
to shape it, to open his mouth, only to have that beginning mistaken for
a sign-language request for directions to the men's john:

The man with the word took a table near the door
And felt the pulse pushing up through the floor.
He opened his mouth in the shape of the word,
But before the night air in him could come out to say,
The bartender nodded and pointed that way.

Some time back, a friend of mine, he's dead now, asked me why I had put the artist in the "shit house," as he called it. And then before I had time to tell him, or to find an in-character way of denying that a question had been asked, he accused me of having a childishly dirty mind and a nihilistic attitude toward art. By the time he finished I could see that he was immensely pleased with how well he'd been able to call me a lot of fancy names for pretty rotten things. He looked so pleased with himself that, knowing how seldom he felt that way, I helped him along with more bad names I'd remembered Mr. Kringle using on Arden Murphy, the eleven-year-old boy who got sent away until he was twenty-one. "Take your hands out of your pockets, boy," Mr. Kringle used to say to Arden. "What are you playing with down there?" Or, passing through the boys' toilet room after supper, "How long does it take you to make a bowel movement in there, boy? Stand up, let's see your sticky fingers, boy—put 'em out, boy, put 'em out." And then Mr. Kringle would go on with dirty names spoken in German, which to me made them sound a lot dirtier, like something you couldn't hire anybody to fish out of the plumbing. Well, I presented a lot of those names and some others I made up on the spot to my friend, who's dead now, and after a while he said, "Weismann, you're pulling my leg." And I said that if he just stopped and thought about it for a little while he'd realize that that was a pretty dirty thing to say, too.

No, I wasn't spoiling to say "potty" at the dinner table. I did that in season very long ago, before I broke my nose the first time, and I was four when that happened. I was thinking—back there in Florence, Italy in the winter of 1962 when I wrote that artist into the men's john—I was thinking more like what the Reverend William Clebsch was thinking when he gave that Christmas sermon at the Church of the Good Shepherd in Austin, Texas. "Look well around you," he said, "at this congregation— for the one thing of which we my be sure about a Second Coming of Our Lord is that it will happen in the most unlikely place." Like the Reverend Clebsch, I wanted to be reminded—and to remind—that the extraordinarily expected often happens in extraordinarily unexpected places. Who would have expected, for instance, that had they walked into that abandoned football stadium in Chicago on December 2, 1942, they would have walked into the first nuclear chain reaction?

My man with the word wanted that word to be heard; that's his whole role: to carry the word, to put it into the air—all over, anywhere, and to have it heard and understood. And he is untiring: look at the places he goes searching for that hearing ear and understanding heart. So then he's misdirected, *maybe,* by a bartender to the men's john. So, what's so odd about that, I say.

I remember racing my brand new, white, 1940 Plymouth convertible with a special twelve-inch speaker under the dash, all the way from Bloomington to Rossville, Illinois, just to see Margaret Foster for an hour and then turn around and race back. For miles I had to pee, but couldn't afford the time. But when I got to the sign at the edge of town that said ROSSVILLE, the slanted stroke of the "R" had been painted out, and the "O" changed to a "U" and I laughed so hard at eighty miles an hour that I began to wet my pants.

At the first bar in Rossville, I stopped, hopped out, went in, ordered a beer and asked, "Where's the washroom?"

"Right here," the bartender said.

"Right *where?"* I asked in pain.

"Right here," he said, knocking his knuckles against a copper sink right in plain open sight behind the bar.

"Right *there?"*

"What's the matter, ain't it good enough for you?" he snarled, looking out the window at that brand new convertible with the radio still playing. "Okay," I said. "Okay, I guess I've come farther than I thought."

So I walked around the end of the bar, stood at the sink and reached for my zipper.

That's as far as I got. The bartender swung at me, yelling, "Why, you goddamn filthy son-of-a-bitchin' pervert, you—!"

I went up and over the bar, through the screen door and into that Plymouth and didn't stop until I was out the other side of Rossville. It may seem strange to some, but I never thought that my experience in Rossville was odd or dirty. It was unexpected, to be sure, but odd, no. All that bartender and I had between us was a language difficulty. He knew well enough, and perhaps for his whole long life, that a "washroom" is where you wash, not pee. I should have asked for the men's room, the john, the gents', the can, the toilet. I just had the wrong word, but, by the gods, I was open to the unexpected.

You see, to give the plot away, our man with the word is headed for showdown in that can in the back of that St. Louis saloon:

By a force not quite his own, and stronger it seemed,
He rose from the table and went where he'd been pointed.
There in the back where the backroom boys could be having a ball,
A painter was painting at a converted confessional.
With his feet planted wide apart, he worked on a canvas
Nailed to the flat back of the dead magic stall.
The roof over the middle was gone, as if something inside had blown up,
Or something from outside had blown down.
The one-way cloth to left and right was rent away by time and breath,
The swinging doors, unswung, revealed the worm-holey seat, filled
With fidgets and little dark spots as deep as the plank.

"And why," someone like my dead friend might ask, "is the artist using a confessional for an easel?" The first time I ever really looked at that piece of architectural furniture called a confessional, was right after I'd spent an hour standing in front of Masaccio's *Holy Trinity* in the church of Santa Maria Novella in Florence in the fall of 1961. I'd looked very hard at that great fresco and it had looked back very hard at me, and I wanted to sit down. The closest place was a confessional against the same wall, a little toward the altar, and for a split second I thought of sitting down in it. Then I realized that that would be most unsuitable and I just stood there looking at it.

The longer I looked, the more it be came clear to me that I'd never really *seen* a confessional before. The one I was looking at must have been pretty old, maybe fifty or seventy-five years, and worn. Like so many others, it echoed the basic plan of the basilica—a nave and two aisles. The larger central area, for the priest or bishop, was flanked by two smaller, more open areas for the penitent. I wondered if this plan was intended to care for the possibility of the priest or bishop hearing two confessions at once, or, if during especially busy times, there would be two priests or bishops, or one of each in the center space listening to two penitents at the same time. The confessional I was looking at there in Santa Maria Novella had two free-swinging doors to the central area, like old-time Western saloon doors, but much lower. Above the doors there was a black draw-curtain, and that morning the curtain was to one side so I could look in. Inside there was a narrow shelf on which, I presumed, the priest or bishop or both sat. This shelf or bench was not very wide, and it seemed to me that if two priests or two bishops, or one of each were hearing confessions at the same time, they would both have to be rather thin. This seemed possible since Santa Maria Novella is a church of the Dominican order, and Dominican priests or bishops with their scholarly intellectualism might be presumed to be thinner than Augustinians, for instance. Above the bench and at the level of the face of a seated, average-size man, there were two fabric-covered openings to left and right toward the positions for penitents. The fabric was light in color and perhaps cotton.

When I finally sat down in the priest's or bishop's position and closed the draw-curtains, I found I could see light coming from the direction of the entrance to the church and discern the moving shapes of people between me and the light. When I looked in from the penitent's position I couldn't see a thing since I was looking into darkness. One of the pieces of fabric was torn, a three- or four-inch rent, and I wondered how that had happened, but I wondered more why it hadn't been sewed up or replaced. The bench of the central area was of hard wood, as was the whole confessional, and, except for the color and the varnish, it reminded me of the seats in the bleachers of the old Marquette University stadium in Milwaukee. There weren't any initials or messages carved in the confessional bench, but it was deeply scarred and spotted. I wondered about that, but attributed it to vandals. But I wondered who they might have been and when they'd done it. At night? When the church was full of people, like at Easter? Sometime like the twenty-sixth of April in 1478 when Pope Sixtus IV, Archbishop Salviati and some of the Pazzi gang managed to stab Giuliano dé Medici to death and cut up Lorenzo in the cathedral right there in town? During the war when the Allies bombed out the railroad station across the street? By those soldiers billeted there in one war or another? Would a priest or a bishop take a whack at that bench or carve it up a little? I remember feeling that if Iwere a priest or bishop listening over and over, year after year, to the recitation of the same old sins, I'd perhaps whack the bench an awful lot, and maybe do quite a bit of carving to pass the time.

There wasn't any roof over the confessional there in Santa Maria Novella and it sat about a foot and a half from the wall. The back was flat and undecorated, except for the number three drawn beautifully in white chalk, and I thought what a fine surface it would be to paint on—especially to back-up large pieces of unstretched canvas: just nail up a good big piece and go to work on that very solid, stable support. When I thought of that, I thought back to the Masaccio painting just about thirty feet from the confessional, and thoughts of art and religion got to running fast in me.

I thought of Masaccio, no more than twenty-six years old when he painted the *Holy Trinity,* and by his gifts subjecting the Father, Son, Holy Ghost, Mary and St. John to the discoveries and mysteries of a scientific perspective. I thought of this young Italian scaling the Trinity to the exact size of the Italians who first saw it that way five and a half centuries ago in this very fresco. I thought of Masaccio subjecting the Holy Trinity to the ordinary limitations of the clock in this natural image of fixed time and fixed position. I thought of him helping to crumble the vigorous medieval church with this visual manifesto of scientific humanism. I thought of the flashy realistic heathenism of Raphael contracted by the Pope for fleshing out in the Signature Room of the Vatican, and of Michelangelo painting a bellybutton on Adam made in the image of God the Father, now flying on the ceiling of the Sistine Chapel. And I thought of all those chalk diagrams I watched being drawn on a pavement one night in Toronto—drawn in rhythm to a coughing voice intent on proving the fallacy of the Immaculate Conception and the tyranny of the Mother Church. But mostly I thought of my own painting, and of whatever there was in me that could be called religious. I walked back the thirty-feet to the Masaccio fresco and knew for sure that I wished I had a confessional for my very own—to use as an easel.

The man with the word stood at the corner where easel and
    confessional met,
And, staring at the border of end and beginning, drew a deep breath.
But instead of the word, a great block came and constipated the man
    with pain;
He fell to the floor and rolled, kicked and thrashed and moaned,
While the painter, painting still, eased him around to the easel side
Where, in the light of the backroom glow, the painting showed.

In 1958 I stopped to see Lee Malone, then director of the Houston Museum of Fine Arts. He was on the phone and said he'd be with me in a few minutes. I walked out toward one of the galleries where a sign said there was an exhibition of paintings by Nicolas de Stael. I knew a little of his work, mostly through reproductions, and almost nothing of the man. I hadn't come to see the exhibition, I hadn't even known it was showing. I put out my cigarette at the entrance to the gallery and then looked up. There ahead of me about twenty feet was a small painting, maybe twenty-four by thirty inches, and with my first look I felt that I'd been stopped in mid-air. Quiet it was, with grayed pinks and a velvety black that opened up forward and back and into the whole world. I stood there feeling a great thing happening, and later I knew that it had. For three or four years after that, much of the world I lived in was the world of that painting, *The Beach at Honfleur*. For years almost every painting I made, and almost every one I tried to make, was another case of trying to repaint that one of de Stael's. The one that came closest, although perhaps no one but I knows or could recognize its lineage, was one I called *War Storage*, with grayed pinks and bulky black tarpaulin-covered shapes on a beach, that today reminds me as much of the beach from which I was evacuated from the South Pacific as it does of de Stael's. A few years ago I wrote the full title on the back. so I'd be sure never to forget: *War Storage: Homage to de Stael.*

The man with the word looked up from the pulsing floor,
Into the yellow-gold, white on black vermilion, green to blue and

Clear through the placeless space filled with images moving, never
    still
Full of the tides of eyes and seas, the weather of rocks and bones,
An infinite field in a single flower of life-as-life continuous.

In 1956 I saw Jackson Pollock's painting, *Number 1,* the one with the
finely interwoven skeins of black and blue and white, and the flecks of
red looking like peering through a barbed wire barricade and torn lace,
with his handprints in the upper right—the one that hangs at 11 West
53rd Street in New York. Stanza sixty-seven may say all I can say in the
right way about that painting as an end and maybe a beginning. It was
the only painting I was recalling as that stanza was being written while it
rained in Florence that winter day in 1962.

There on that piece of canvas, the painter's sudarium, was wiped
    afresh
The color of lost surprise, the face of first encounter.
There the infinitely distanced multitudes and varieties were patterned
In a life-size sensuous replica of the fated everlasting force
That winds and binds absolute and relative in wordless space and time.
And the man who called it by the name of jelly, lost the word like the
    ghost
As the block gave way and the pain flew with the sight.

Nicolas de Stael may have jumped off the Eiffel Tower on St. Patrick's
Day, and Jackson Pollock turned himself over in an Oldsmobile 88, but
The Beach at Honfleur and *Number 1* remain with all the heritage that
gathers as a single voice to call us back to ourselves.

"In childhood we live under the brightness of immortality—
heaven is as near and actual as the seaside. Behind the complicated details of the world stand the simplicities: God is good, the
grown-up man or woman knows the answer to every question,
there is such a thing as truth, and justice is as measured and fault-

less as a clock. Our heroes are simple: they are brave, they tell the truth, they are good swordsmen, and they are never in the long run really defeated. That is why no later books satisfy us like those which were read to us in childhood—for those promised a world of great simplicity of which we knew the rules, but the later books are complicated and contradictory with experience; they are formed out of our own disappointing memories . . . we cannot recognize the villain and we suspect the hero and the world is a small cramped place. The two great popular statements of faith are What a small place the world is and I'm a stranger here myself."*

Far off a wooden owl on a cornice of a courthouse hooted,
A child felt warm in a coop a little back from Tillamook;
Flowers bloomed in an innerspring mattress in Natchez, while a bell
Tolled one among the Los Angeles graveyard junk,
And a word on a raft blew down in the rivers' Y.

*Graham Greene, *The Ministry of Fear*, Penguin, 1970, p.95.

JELLY WAS THE WORD

1.
Jelly, he said, and no one got the word,
Not even gooseflesh in the backdraft.

2.
Jelly was the word as surely as
A fair ball batted backwards
Is foul.

3.
The word was his to voice abroad
In hopes it could be heard by anyone
In certainty or doubt,
Dungarees or double-breasted pinstripes,
Robed in worms or cloth or naked
In wisdom or ignorance, stretching to marvel
The excarnation of the hooded false.

4.

When the sun came out, stripped as Greek mythology in Basic
   Esperanto,
He formed the word full in the leeside air of a hill
Upstream so it would carry the load of tidings down
Almost according to the local weather prediction, and maybe
Get through to the most unsuspecting.
But those about were in mezzo-humanist chorus
With anvils, tongs and sledges
Beating out shoes for plaster casts of deep-freeze Parthenon horses
While singing to keep their ears pragmatically deaf.
He funneled the word down and lofted it on high,
But unhearing they went about their copyrighted schedule to noon
When they kidnapped a child in effigy, the daily ritual
For keeping the curriculum from jeopardy
And untowardness.

5.

At five, by a timepiece ignited by a dead President
From the bowl of fire at the Olympics,
They queued up to a shake or trill and galloped behind
An overlapping spur,
While his last trumpeted jelly came hallooing back from the hills
   around,
Unsullied and unheard.

6.

Yelling jelly into the wind, for who knows where
A dark-adapted protectively colored wayfaring intimate
May bend his ear,
He rode the rods below the oldest reefer of the Nickel Plate
To night in Cleveland's yard.

7.
Where the tracks brake-shine under
The ferro-concrete arch named nineteen-oh-nine,
Big and square in a recessed panel,
He eased from his knees to the gravel
And headed beneath the bridges for the square below the tower
Built with a lot of hard arms and stolen bilk carried unclean
To the top in a hod with a perforated bottom
That failed to drain away the filth.

8.
Night in the bilious grass of the square,
Criss-crossed with suicidewalks,
Sucked out bunches of hoarheads mixed
With the young defeated in their own success.
They stood around in slipknots wearing tin
Question marks arguing for no stakes between chewing.

9.
In the stop-watched seconds when every body was silent,
Chewing or thumbnailing their far back teeth at once,
There was nothing but the weak din of the place
That could be sliced by voice easier than amber light the fog.
And in those seconds they stood between
Blank and tense, looking the same, but smelling different
To foxes and everything hunted.
Among them there was a brand of waiting
As if they'd been hurt in the gaps of their reason,
And to bridge the wound had found
A whipping-goat to flail with a swipple loaded with nails
And drive to trial for defecation of their undecipherable characters.

10.
In this receptive blank, this
Waiting for waiting, no matter for what,
He who held the word could hope to have it heard,
So he told it through the din, then mushroomed it over the square
Like jelly inside the dome of the planetarium.

11.
One wooden owl with mirror eyes planted
On a cornice of the courthouse
To scare away the chalk-loaded pigeons,
Tried to hoot as the word went out
Unheard, and its flock of echoes bleated away to din and died
As the silent chewing erupted again
In modulated belches and mouth muscle fussings that sounded
Something like but not language.

12.
In a westbound cab driven with abandon
By a moonlighting high school English teacher worried sick
How he'd make ends meet and just barely,
He was carried carrying the word to a bottleneck east of Ashtabula
Where the sign said KNOW YOU TURN and the driver did,
Clear around to N.Y.U.

13.
The last generation of the Institute's early Cinquecentists was
    returning
In an Albertian line from a coffee break in step
With footnotes on arches.
They'd given up the trace of man in paint and stone
Along with cigarettes and rhythm-method humanism,
Too troubled on the one hand by the possibility of abscess
Making the heart grow fonder, and on the other

By the harrowing possibility of flat-out confrontation
With the magnificent Italian dead-end.
Ex post facto architectural theory and oldtime unsymbolic logic
Are two slow fasts they kept to avoid the feast of those
They'd slaughtered in themselves.

14.
They walked the radius of a circular park
After carefully stepping over the circumference,
And assembly-lined their way towards the center
Where he who had the word stood,
A physical block.
Knowing that these professing doctors without patience spoke,
And even understood many languages natively,
He pronounced jelly to them in the standard cultivated manners
Of every language, group and sub-family of
Indo-European, Semetic, Finno-Ugric, Dravidian,
Malayo-Polynesian, Turkic, Monogolic, Sino-Tibetan and even
Hokan out of Iroquoian
For that semester's guest in Advanced Etruscan Tub Vaults,
On leave from Princeton and Columbia.
It got into their pores, nostrils and navels,
Their ears, mouths and all aperatures south;
Their teeth, suet, bones and nails,
But it died there, all
Sundered and unheard.

15.
Pushing down the narrow-gauge spasms of their constricted discipline,
They packed up so tight at the compass-pricked center where he stood
That they broke wee puffs of vestigial kamikaze, pre-soured
In the caustic channels of their inner dark.

16.
Outraged by the frustration of their one-track blight-of-way
To the second radius, that if traversed to the circumference
Would give them a whole diameter to their scholarly credit,
They dispatched the most compulsive of the squeezed
Out of the obfuscation to the Bell System to phone
For civil liberties.

17.
The piewagon came full of New York's Finest in new jerseys.
The one with the longevity and double veteran's preference
Invited the word-carrying one inside and he asked why,
Only to be told that it looked like disorderly breach
In a public with no visible means, but
That was a matter for the bench.
When they began to push him in that way
That looks like overly demonstrative brotherly love from the outside,
But feels like valet service mixed with judo and sacked beebees inside,
A small boy with an olive slingshot standing on a hydrant
Said it would be false arrest because
One of the flatfeet was out of uniform, and
Quite suddenly he was released.

18.
Freely bound, then, on his quest for a hearing ear, and giving
To the probability that the word might go forth better inside than out,
He hitched his hopes to a star going west, like
Columbus, but a little more south.
Near the Rio Guadalupe he unhitched and hiked
Through derrick-shaded cotton fields and grasslands studded
With saltlicks and horn-brimmed spectacles
On four legs walking,
Into Victoramus of the Lonesome Star.

19.
There on the main street where it most likely would be
In a town squared off around the courthouse jail,
The bank stood looking like a camouflaged safe keeping guard
Over its assorted but negotiable insides.
Through the goldleaf-lettered, plateglass door he went
With an air conditioned by purpose to a rose marble room where
Cattlemen came to trade winds and stock their accounts
While mostly hitting the double fluted gold bicuspidors.

20.
In the fortune projected beyond Mercator for him, he arrived
To the fanfare of the empty room, and
Took position for unleashing the word
From silence.

21.
While the 33 1/3 r.p.m. platter of recorded electronic bell sounds
Played out the blinded arcades of the phony
Belfry of the Refundamentalistic steeple,
Only to tell time what it already knew,
The cattlemen came dragging their kale behind them.
They hunkered down to trade and borrow
And write notes to the promissory land.
By nicatating and tonguing their cheeks they signaled
The branded hides to change range and hands
Across the taut barbed wire.

22.
Without a sound among the hunkered and one,
Except the almost imperfectible tick
Of the time-lock on the Swiss-movement safe,
And the humming of the cowboy spittoon,
He pealed out the word

Gloriously free in the marble room.
The acoustics were chambered like a nautilus encouraging
The air to perfect vibrations of audible articulations
Corresponding exactly to the letters of the law
And the syllables of the word
Which should have exported the import
Through sensation to the hunkered, but
All that went returned converted to
Unregenerative feedback that bladdered his gall
As memory and not a call.
Undismayed, he mooed and snorted the word, and
Whinneyed and brayed it ass-like around the cattlemen,
All to the same dissolute end.

23.
As on every day in every week, except Sunday when
They played the other game with the lamb,
They went about their silent business in the marble room
As if alone without themselves, unconscious
Of what they did to pay or rob, but doing
It like ritual unconceived, half in dumb neglect
And half in awful vengeance.

24.
The little click that crawled across the wall
Issued from the time-lock pinching tight for overnight,
Signaling the session's end.
Trading their last scents and dollaring up their accounts,
Like sleeves the raveled care,
They amblingly unhunkered for the door.

25.
Once more he intoned the word while the bought sold and slaughtered
Grazed or bled in grass or profusion far from their executors,

Free as stray swine in the county without a hogreeve.
The word splashed jelly on their shirt-fronts, bags of their pants,
Over their naked faces, spread on the ceiling and walls,
Then glacéd the marble floor. Unheard.

26.
Halfway to the filigree porch
He sensed an ideal acoustical balance between spaces
Open and closed like time ajar in the fruit cellar,
And he laid out the word in a horizontal wall
At the level of their departing ears.
It ran around the globe, an earlevel Heaviside layer laving
The pinna, meatus and tympanum,
Then splayed lost in the labyrinth.

27.
Along the street paved with dust and darkness,
The evening paper came out biased at the seams precisely on time,
And he looked for the lost and found help-wanted personals
In the ads of the have-not.
No one, nor even a tax-whelped corporation,
Syndicate or extremely non-profit foundation garment
For the founder's unction bed was advertising a lust
Or a hunch for hearing.
So, wistfully, there on the dark corner
Where east meets west and north and south to boot,
He watched the kipling down of the town
Into no dreams it had not had.

28.
In the morning,
A little back from Tillamook Bay
Near the pioneers' museum, a child
Playing with a plastic tongue-blade and parts of a pop-up toaster,

Looked his way when he said jelly,
But his mother, harried and wary,
Pulled him back into a narrow coop where
A cock crew and something heavy fell.

29.
One other light of recognition did flicker
In the opal eyes of a girl certified as mad
By a kind of pick-up band acting as a kangaroo court
One night near Natchez when things were dull, and all
The playing cards were stuck together with cruor.
She appeared to hear the word, and weakly
Rasped the dormant nerve a little, just before
Her spoils-system attendant cuffed her far left of crippled
And smothered her under an inner-spring mattress
Behind the tall unwindowed bars.

30.
Where the red green and gold lay the deepest along the Olentangy,
Out beyond the beating drum-shaped stadium
And the cemetery begun as a Confederate prison,
He saw two lovers through a sycamore screen.
In the Saturday afternoon sun, with the town siphoned off
Into the billion-dollar football bowl,
They lay there almost alone in Franklin County.
The breeze was from someplace filled
With honeysuckle, frankincense and murmur,
To which they added musk, a trace of fingerling and sighs
They shed their clothes and stabled their cares
And made each in the other's image inseparable,
Wrapped, spathed and spermed anaesthetized.
The moving shadows wrote them in the leaves
And they answered in the last of the sun.
They rose regenerate to a world still at their ease,

And while it held he floated out the word,
Only to pass around and through them;
A light unseen,
A time unkept.

31.
Along his way to the coast
Where the memory of the old oaken Arkies still rapes the path,
He called the word up to a hole in the library facade
Where an Arizona grackle was
Being shot for lunch by a bibliographer.
As the bird fell into the awning below,
The bibliographer leaned out mumbling that:
The first copy, Celery King Collection, acquired from Mogol Flatt,
Is one of six known in original wrappers with all points
Plus inserted four-leaf clover, but reconstructed and
Spine title so pasted that it now heads up.

32.
Just in case the bibliographer was using his mouth to repudiate his ears,
He called the word up the wall between breaths,
Only to have it pushed back with a recitation that:
The Jenny Wren Version is in original condition, possibly
Of black cloth as reported by Heartman and Canny,
And of an issue which,
Like those before and after,
Incorporates some no-name as well as Craghead and slip titles, and
That if the report is unverified and the variant discovered
Only in green cloth it should be
Reclassified as 3b (issue 3, variant impression 3).

33.
Some swallows homing from Wyoming flew south
While the bibliographer kept spewing his diarrheal down
The classicistic wall by incremental repetition,
And the man with the word walked away west
To the outskirts of Los Angeles.

34.
There, before the expressway begins to be what it expressly is,
He paused at the hubcap crusted gate that gave
To a hundred-acre automotive Forest Lawn.
The sun was burning on the other side of the earth,
Blocked out by the crust, moho and molten core,
But the blackened sky behind the graveyard was caught in the crossfire
Of the Auroras Borealis and Australis and it flickered
Fitfully in a barrage of sheet steel lightning.
The once worshiped graveyard junk gave back
Chromium lights from the bloodpoisonous dark
Hovering close among the grease-cold unhooded heads,
Toothless flywheels flown dead into the back transmission cavity,
Fractured shock-absorbent arms, shocked their last by the lost road,
    hanging
Under the unhinged jaws of girder-booms in once one-piece frames
    and skeletons,
Litters now for exploded doors, undriven shafts, unsteered wheels
    galore;
Universals manifolded, bent twisted, cracked and broken waiting
The clarion call to shrapnel in the next somewhat limited war.
Here and there the angled iron was hung with upholstery crape
    moving
Ominously as Georgia Spanish moss in May
Through flake-edged saws of safety glass.
Between the closed-out open hearses, the oiled loam lay
Strewn with spring leaves and visors for the sun,

Bristling cold with brasted fuel-injection pumps,
Pistons, needle valves, gaskets, shims, handles, hinges
And non-armorial ballbearing escutcheons aping heraldry.

35.
The moon went under and the rats peeked out;
They left their nests in dried-out liquid clutches
And collapsed synthetic seats still half stuffed
With plastic straw and crumbs, to search abroad for sustenance
And openings for fever, tularemia, typhus, rabies and plague.
To the north an angelus sounded three and three and nine,
Then nine and three and three undoing.

36.
Through the gate he went along the rutted way of delivery and salvage,
Far to the back against a cyclone-fenced hill
Where a blacked-out cut-rate pay-as-you-go abortion clinic was
Operating full-blast in practiced caution.
The German shepherd, asleep full of rats, was chained to a generator
Fitted with an obliterated brand-name in red and fleur-de-lys.
There were little sighs from inside the tin sign lean-to,
And something like ozone from shock treatments in the air.
The television program, on base in the cubical filled with waiting,
Was moving in six near-middle grays
Backed up with muted juke-Bached catechism preludes
While the well-tempered cleaver and absorbent cotton worked
In the padded induction room beyond.

37.
He cast his eyes through a gash in the Clabber Girl sign,
Past the polyethylene sink to the war-surplus hospital unit inside
Where the work was being done on an olive drab rack.
The one in charge in a barber's coat had been a triple-threat man,
Voted All-American Second Team, the first ever

From the College of the Maculate on its drive
To national recognition and fiscal solvency.
He'd not been good enough for pro-ball, so he'd tried insurance
Until he heard about visions from the printed testimony
Of a State's Evidence Witness against a Harvard graduate
Accused of aiding and abetting the red homonculus.
Helped by an old head injury inflicted during a homecoming game
    years before,
He drank himself to his own sure-fire vision, realized
In a rebuilt Trailways bus with enormous tent and Hammond organ,
Driven, pitched and played to evilangelize from border to border
    until death
By strangulation of his male organ player cost him all
His new gained wealth, reputation as a healer,
And eight years in the pen.
His pen-pals advised the junk-pusher's trade, but once out,
He turned, rather, to this graveyard procuring of premature delivery.

38.
Now, framed in the gash and obviously at the end of the night's
    agenda,
He was washing and wringing his hands in the sink.
Then, still with the towel, he collapsed
Into the tubular chair at the plastic-topped table and dropped
His head on his folded arms with an agonizing groan.

39.
In the consummate silence that resumed, and musing
How the stars at noon come out from the bottom of the pit,
The man with the word voiced it clearly through the gash in the tin.
It went straight home to the one in the barber's coat
And he rose up in stark naked fright, there
At the end of his camouflaged nightmare.
While his drums still beat with the waves of the word,

And the one who'd given it backed away from the wall,
He reached for the desperate ace in the panic hole
And pushed the button of his last but one resort.

40.
The circuit, by his final unfree act,
Ringed through the trigger to the charge
Of the nine-pound fragmentation bomb,
And for an instant between none and after-image,
Incandescence bloomed in a corner of the graveyard,
Then gave the vacuum back to the rush of darkness
In a rain of junk on junk and rag and bone.

41.
Only the rats far out from the epicentrum.
Squealed a requiem in life,
And a toad or a dog, someplace,
Strained out an erotic chord.

42.
The one with the word looked away from nothing
Toward the tar-seamed road where the trucks run east,
Lighting the pole-tops and canyon floors
All the winding way to mile-high Denver.

43.
There, after breakfast, he stood on the shoulders of a regential statue,
In situ at the intersection of every concrete path leading
To every clock-wired classroom of an accredited university.
He watched the old children, female and male,
Follow the drawing-board lines like fenced troughs
To their sheep-dip catalogue-described eight o'clock classes.
The deodorized girls were dressed in magazine photographs open
    down the front,

Carrying their transistor books and pancake bags casually
As they walked caressing themselves in nylon sandwiches out of sight.
The boys, bereft now of subsidized juvenile delinquency, and adrift
Between recollections of pre-puberty and carte blanche anticipation,
Were thumbing their way to the suck-in of some organizational
　　claque
Where, relieved of responsibility for their acts, should they dare,
Could some day soon dandle the oscillations of their erotomania
On an expense account while doing what's necessary only
To provide statistics in support of a long deceased fiction.

44.

The grass had been cut and rolled by tandem power mowers,
The brick and stone courses tuck-pointed that spring;
The windows were washed and shaded adroitly with pastel blinds,
All under a fleece-wisped sky so deep and high
It took more than the naked eye to find the vapor streaming
Behind the military budget, just before the sonic booms.

45.

From this high place of vantage, straddling the close-spaced ears
Of the regent unremembered though cast in bronze way before the
　　day he died,
The one with the word filled his lungs with the colloquial
Air of the place and broke forth the word through the unexpecting
　　hum.
Its crested waves were seismographic and little inked needles around
　　the world
Charted the duo-syllable jelly, just so, on paper rolls and drums.
But its sound, if to them at all, lay on the land
Like the sound of a bell made of meat.

46.
With no more adieu than the day is lost going west
Across the line on the other side of the Great Plains beginning,
They went their sequestered ways, some to bingo-jargon games
    played with ponies
And some few to non-sequiturial lectures full of perspectives by
    incongruity.
At ten minutes to nine precisely, and by a Pavlov bell multiplied,
They made the doors and steps back to the concrete belts, and on
To the half-circle clearing under the Tudor windows of the Vice
    President
Where they demonstrated, minuet-like, about certain campus parking
    restrictions.

47.
The mousy faculty judges, appointed by the paranoiac dean,
Sat after an engraving of Raphael's *Disputa* on a balcony hung over
The exactly prescribed student demonstration area,
To score by points on square tagboard grids, easily fitted to the lap,
The comparative degrees of decorum as defined
In the regentially prepared and newly re-tied Hand and Foot Book
    for Students;
And as manifested by the various Greek letter groups
Of the Pan-Hellenic Society during this particular demonstration
Now ending on time, four minutes before nine.

48.
The winning group, a sorority whose strategy had been passive
    assistance,
Was present only by proxy in the person of the sorority father who
Happened, also, to be the paranoiac dean.
He was outrageously applauded by his self-appointed judges
As they presented to every member of the sorority, in absentia,
A gold-stamped, top-grained cowhide slip-on cover

For their personal prints of the Hand and Foot Book.
After the Pan-Hellenic hymn was sung, and a maintenance man on
  the roof
Ran the Decorum Flag up to the soft underside of Old Glory,
The President of the Senior Class led them in collective unconscious
  meditation,
While the vines quietly clawed their way up the wall.

49.
From his perch on the dead regent's bronze pate,
In the still of twenty-seven seconds to nine,
The man with the word loosed it loud again and then attended
The echo's funeral procession all along the ring around
The Rockies' pocket full of mile-high Denver.

50.
Somewhere in cellars or bunkers far back and under,
Some other students may have been plotting toward truthfulness,
But their retreats kept out as well as in,
So what they did and said was as dead without
As jelly was within.

51.
Over a ridge where a path falls down in Maryland,
The man with the word angled his way to Camp Pinkerton,
Named for Allan the cooper who foiled the Molly Maguires, and
Kept Old Abe from being shot until Booth did it in a box
And Allan's sons went a-scabbing in May with labor spies.

52.
The pup and top-dog tents were neat in row on row,
(Oh gently down the scream with a PX whisky wash),
Well away from the officers' mansions covered
With masonry hors d'oeuvres and rank flags flying

In the slipstream of another smokescreen investigation,
Involving low candlepower in the mess hall and shower,
Trumped up to wet-blanket the red-hot charges
Of brutality to the literates refusing to use in time of peace
The toilet articles of war.

53.
Hard by the electric picket fence, where
A sign shouted out PEACE IS OUR PROFESSION—SLEEP WELL TONIGHT,
The motor pool stood shimmering with rockets
Rigged up as bookmobiles and ambulances.
The half-track bicycles, bought on a southern contract just before
    election,
Were lined up smart before the amphibious baby carriages
Loaded with gesundheit bazookas and four-in-hand grenades.
The high flung command cars with mohair seats were back
From a Colonel-and-up safari in New Nations Africa,
With side trips to the Western Indies and ex-French Asia,
And they lined the mall through the center of the pool
Draped with trophies and form letters from off-Central Intelligence.
Between the ram-jam radiation bulldozers, uncontaminated earth
    spreaders,
Troop-dropping trucks and mobile missile planters, a Private First
    Class
Was reaming the tail-pipes free of carbon vacuously
When the man with the word hissed jelly through the fence.
The Private kept reaming as if dreaming of the metaphors
He was mixing, and pointed blank to the mess hall yonder.

54.
The siren way up the water tower bewailed the loss of morning,
And half a division of non-commissioned flowers of youth
Anthologized at the steam tables of their mid-day meal.
At the decibel height of the uncushioned mess hall clatter,

When seven and half thousand were in a single sight,
The cocky chicken-Colonel appeared in starch and brass at the open
   front door,
Flanked by two West-Pointed Majors and a pair of VMI Captains to
   keep the score,
He cued-in the command that wracked the hall in tiers of attention
And laid away the last living sound in the fresh-created mausoleum.
Into this erectilinear solid of silence, and before the next regular
   command,
The man with the word sent it forth in a blast of sound that
   resounded
From every atom in every molecule of solid, liquid and gas.
But the half-division of men with a full division of ears
Stood as a single frozen stone,
Numbed deeper into dumbness by blind respect and fear
Of the uniformed team-shaped myth, mythically champing at a
   glorious bit.

55.
He left Pinkerton while the shadows were still underfoot, and
   overhead
An ornithopter owned by a Puerto Rican ad agency, trailed a fretwork
   sign
That read EMIT NWO RUO NI EVOL SI YTIRUCES LAICOS from the north,
And from the south: SOCIAL SECURITY IS LOVE IN OUR OWN TIME.

56.
That night, between the tarnished gold coast and the flaming skies of
   Gary,
He watched the thousands go in guilt-edged boredom,
Curiosity, ignorance and emptiness
Down the streets and through the concrete holes
Into Chicago's Soldier Field,
To see and hear Young Billy Migraine,

The crusading self-evaginist, go vertigo and hypnotize
Half a hundred thousand with himself on snowbird snuff,
About a no-down-payment Jesus who consecretes the status quo.

57.
Thinking of great numbers and the scatter of probability for almost
  anything,
The man with the word filed in with the mob to a seat on the fifty-
  yard line.
High on the rim of the Field, under the moonless sky by the lake,
He watched Young Billy career in his checkered coat and movie face,
Right down to the semi-final when he called
For a hundred thousand safety matches to be lit
To prove his light in mob psychology darkness.
And while the matches burned in something like noiselessness,
The man with the word thundered it out, then shrieked it staccato;
But not a match died out, nor was a voice borne high or low
Until Young Billy Migraine called for personally autographing Jesus
To the music of electric guitars.

58.
The sky threw up, and the man with the word
Went by a side gate to the open road
Past places that still await their names,
To Billings on the Yellowstone.

59.
Along the river where the outcropping prehistoric remains,
A Memphis gambling outfit was working hard in its carnival guise
To get to Great Falls in the clear.
The snag-numbered wheels and skin games with five-sided bones
Were slicing the deficit when a Blackfoot and a Kootenai too
  suddenly fleeced,
Lashed the debonair concessionaire to the other side of his birthday

With smartly matched lacings from straps of plaited thong and
    horsehair.
The man with the word had witnessed it all,
So the Billings police took him off to one side
To get his statement of what had happened before and after the brawl.
Tell us, they said, in your very own words, how it went pell-mell to
    melee;
And the man said he needed only one to tell, and that one was jelly.
The Sergeant said he'd better be careful, sir,
About withholding an officer and resisting evidence,
But the man kept answering with jelly, loud and clear,
Until the Sergeant took his fingerprints and turned him over to the
    State Patrol
In their souped-up Mercury with automatic guns in the upholstery
    they told him,
By damn, he sounded like one of those liberals from Eastern
    Montana State Normal,
So forthwith they sped him into the Bitterroot Range
And dumped him hard in a gray ghost town.

60.
On a raft of shingles, clapboards and saloon doors,
He floated away from Three Forks, down the Missouri,
Across the plains of North and South Dakota,
Nebraska, Kansas, Iowa and Missouri, calling jelly all the way
Along the river and into Bismark, Pierre, the City of the Sioux,
Council Bluffs, Omaha, Atchison, Leavenworth and Kansas City,
    clear
To the Father of Waters, seventeen miles above Saint Louis.

61.
He beached his raft where the waters meet and watched them prove
    they were one.
With a brush of river rushes and paint of the brightest clay,

He lettered out the word as a sign on the darkened raft
And stood it against an oak growing gray in the waters' Y.
He walked the tufted banks below the bluffs, the sands
Along the coming peneplain, past the bridges spanning east,
South out of the west to Looey's name-sainted City of the Blues.

62.
He turned with the town away from the river and the cast iron-gated
    fronts
Into streets the flatboatmen and sidewheel trade helped
To plank and cobble below the tar and cement.
A piano was being played by a half-gone son of the Proclamation
Stilted up on a dunnage stand behind the handwrought bar,
Under the neon lights jumping in a jack-knife dive on Rummage
    Street.
The melody was anchored in rhythmic pitch that kept the flukes
    from rusting,
And by the chain he rocked the vessel through the doors of the lock
Between the high morning river and the low down twilight blue.

63.
The man with the word took a table near the door
And felt the pulse pushing up through the floor.
He opened his mouth in the shape of the word,
But before the night air in him could come out to say,
The bartender nodded and pointed that way.

64.
By a force not quite his own, and stronger it seemed,
He rose from the table and went where he'd been pointed.
There in the back where the backroom boys could be having a ball,
A painter was painting at a converted confessional.
With his feet planted wide apart, he worked on a canvas
Nailed to the flat back of the dead magic stall.

The roof over the middle was gone, as if something inside had blown
    up,
Or something from outside had blown down.
The one-way cloth to left and right was rent away by time and breath,
The swinging doors, unswung, revealed the worm-holey seat, filled
With fidgets and little dark spots as deep as the plank.

65.
The man with the word stood at the corner where easel and
    confessional met,
And, staring at the border of end and beginning, drew a deep breath.
But instead of the word, a great block came and constipated the man
    with pain;
He fell to the floor and rolled, kicked and thrashed and moaned,
While the painter, painting still, eased him around to the easel side
Where, in the light of the backroom glow, the painting showed.

66.
The man with the word looked up from the pulsing floor,
Into the yellow-gold, white on black vermilion, green to blue and
Clear through the placeless space filled with images moving, never still,
Full of the tides of eyes and seas, the weather of rocks and bones,
An infinite field in a single flower of life-as-life continuous.

67.
There on that piece of canvas, the painter's sudarium, was wiped afresh
The color of lost surprise, the face of first encounter.
There the infinitely distanced multitudes and varieties were patterned
In a life-size sensuous replica of the fated everlasting force
That winds and binds absolute and relative in wordless space and time.
And the man who called it by the name of jelly, lost the word like the
    ghost
As the block gave way and the pain flew with the sight.

68.

Far off a wooden owl on a cornice of a courthouse hooted,
A child felt warm in a coop a little back from Tillamook;
Flowers bloomed in an innerspring mattress in Natchez, while a bell
Tolled one among the Los Angeles graveyard junk,
And a word on a raft blew down in the rivers' Y.